GREAT CITIES

THROUGH THE AGES

LONDON

First American Edition published in 2004
by Enchanted Lion Books
115 West 18th Street, New York, NY 10011

ISBN 1–59270–013–6

LIBRARY OF CONGRESS CATALOGING-IN-PUBLICATION DATA

A CIP record for this book is available from the Library of Congress.

McRae Books Srl
Borgo S. Croce, 8, 50122 — Florence, Italy
info@mcraebooks.com

Text: Neil Morris
Illustrations: Andrea Ricciardi di Gaudesi, Paola Baldanzi, Manuela Cappon,
Lorenzo Cecchi, Lucia Mattioli, Paola Ravaglia, Studio Stalio (Alessandro
Cantucci, Fabiano Fabbrucci, Andrea Morandi, Ivan Stalio)
Graphic Design: Marco Nardi
Layout: Yotto Furuya
Editors: Claire Moore, Anne McRae
Picture Research: Valerie Meek, Claire Moore
Cutouts: Filippo Delle Monache, Giampietro Bruno, Alman Graphic Design
Color Separations: Litocolor, Florence (Italy)

ACKNOWLEDGEMENTS
All efforts have been made to obtain and provide compensation for the
copyright to the photos and artworks in this book in accordance with
legal provisions. Persons who may nevertheless still have claims are
requested to contact the copyright owners.

t=top; tl=top left; tc=top center; tr=top right; c=center; cl=center left;
cr=center right; b= bottom; bl=bottom left; bc=bottom center; br=bottom right

The Publishers would like to thank the following museum for its
permission to publish its images.

12–13b, 25b, 31b, 40tl Courtesy of the Museum of London.

The Publishers would also like to thank the following photographers and
picture libraries for the photos used in this book.

AFP Photo Pool WPA/John Giles: 20c; AFP Photo/Martyn Hayhow: 30br,
42cl; Corbis/Contrasto: 14tl, 15cr, 21tr, 23bc, 29cl, 31tr, 32tr, 32c,
33c, 33b, 34cl, 34bl, 35c, 37c, 37cr, 37b, 38b, 39bl, 42bl, 43bc;
Farabola Foto (The Bridgeman Art Library): 14br, 15b, 16b, 19br, 21cl,
21bc, 24cl, 26–27b, 27tl, 27br, 28cl, The Stapleton Collection 36cl,
39tl, 39cr; Lonely Planet Images: Simon Bracken/LPI 29br, Pat Yale/LPI
30cr, Richard l'Anson/LPI 36b, Neil Setchfield/LPI 37tr, Charlotte
Hindle/LPI 40br, Veronica Garbutt/LPI 41bc, Paul Kennedy/LPI 42br,
43b; Marco Nardi/McRae Books Archives: 5r, 18cl, 22b, 27cr, 31cr;
The Art Archive/Tate Gallery London/Eileen Tweedy: 23cl; The Image
Works: 19tr, 23cr, 25c, 32cl, 33cl, 34br, 35bl, 35c, 41tr, 43c, 43cr.

Printed and bound in Belgium
1 2 3 4 5 / 09 08 07 06 05 04 03

LONDON

Neil Morris

Enchanted Lion Books
New York

The Romans controlled London from around 43 AD until the early 5th century. This 3rd-century mosaic was found in Queen Victoria Street in 1869.

The black cab is a famous sight on London's streets. Mechanically-driven taxis first appeared in London in 1897, and today there are over 17,000 cabs in the city.

Table of Contents

Buckingham Palace, the official London residence of the British monarch, was rebuilt in the early 19th century.

43 AD Romans found Londinium.	**1189** First mayor of London appointed.	Shakespearean theater opens in 1996).	demolished. Christie's, the auctioneers, is founded.	opened by the Prince of Wales.	**1971** New London Bridge is built.

43 AD Romans found Londinium.

c. 200 First city walls built.

886 London comes under the rule of Alfred the Great.

1066 William the Conqueror crowned in Westminster Abbey.

1189 First mayor of London appointed.

1209 First stone London Bridge is completed.

1348–49 The Black Death kills a third of the population.

1599 The Globe Theatre opens. (A replica of this

Shakespearean theater opens in 1996).

1637 Hyde Park is opened to the public.

1666 The Great Fire.

1732 10 Downing Street (prime minister's residence) is acquired by the Crown.

1766 City walls are

demolished. Christie's, the auctioneers, is founded.

1851 The Great Exhibition in Hyde Park.

1863 World's first underground railway opens, from Paddington to Farringdon Road.

1894 Tower Bridge is

opened by the Prince of Wales.

1909 The Victoria and Albert Museum opens.

1940 Severe bomb damage during the Blitz.

1951 The Festival of Britain on the South Bank.

1971 New London Bridge is built.

1981 Docklands development begins.

1994 Eurostar passenger train between London, Paris, and Brussels starts service.

2000 The London Eye opens.

Introduction

Since its foundation nearly two thousand years ago, London has had a remarkable history, full of upheavals and rebirths. Roman invaders created the first settlement on the banks of the River Thames. This quickly grew into a walled city and became a trading port that was highly valued by the Saxons. After Edward the Confessor had made London his royal capital, further great changes came with the Norman invasion of England in 1066. Having been crowned in Westminster Abbey, William the Conqueror built a great protective fortress, the Tower of London. During the Middle Ages the city was governed for the first time by a mayor and his council, and rich merchants and nobles lived in fine houses. Plague, fire, and civil war hit London hard, but also provided the opportunity for a major rebuilding program. This stretched well beyond the original city walls, which were soon pulled down. Mayfair and other districts were filled with fashionable squares, and by 1800 London was the largest city in the world. During the Victorian era, great contrasts existed between the elegant lifestyle of the rich and the desperate situation of the poor. Nevertheless, the English capital continued to grow. Through the 1920s and 1930s, the city experienced widespread urban expansion, as the suburbs of Greater London developed, and the growth of the Underground made commuting a real possibility. During World War II, however, large parts of the city were reduced to rubble and thousands were killed. The post-war period was one of rebuilding and regeneration, as the city recovered from the war. Today, this historic city is home to more than six million people and attracts visitors from all over the world.

Standing 320 feet (98 m) high, Big Ben is one of the most famous landmarks in London.

After the Great Fire of London in 1666, Christopher Wren (above) was one of the most influential architects involved in rebuilding the city.

London suffered widespread destruction during World War II. Thousands of people lost their lives and over a million were made homeless in what became known as the "Blitz."

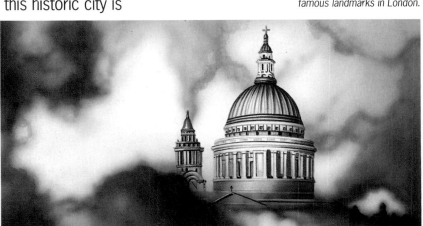

The Britons

In their new province of Britain, the Romans raised wealth by taxing local farmers and traders. As in other provinces, however, the Romanization of different tribes of Celtic Britons varied greatly. Some Celtic chieftains rebelled against Roman rule, while other leaders accepted their new rulers. Most ordinary Britons continued to speak Celtic languages and carried on their own customs and traditional way of life. The Romans were generally happy to allow this.

Above: Bust of the Roman Emperor Claudius, who ruled from 41 to 54 AD.

A family of wealthy Celtic Britons.

6,000 BC – 423 AD

c. 6,000 BC Crops grown, cattle and sheep raised in Britain.

c. 650 BC Celtic languages are introduced to Britain.

55 BC First Roman invasion of Britain, as soldiers land near Deal, in Kent.

54 BC Julius Caesar commands a fleet of 800 ships and 200 Roman cavalry in a second invasion, crossing the River Thames to attack the British commander Cassivellaunus.

27 BC Augustus becomes the first Emperor of Rome.

43 AD Emperor Claudius

Early Roman Settlement

The Roman invading force probably used a floating pontoon bridge to cross the wide, marshy Thames.

Having settled on the north side of the river, some time around 43 AD, they built a more solid bridge and made fortified camps, from which they could protect the new crossing. This was the beginning of Londinium.

Roman iron dagger and sheath found in the Thames.

Londinium

The valley of the River Thames, in southeast England, attracted settlers many thousands of years ago. The region had water, timber, and fertile land. The Romans had first visited the area in 55 BC, but the actual settlement of London only began after 43 AD. In that year about 40,000 Roman troops landed on the coast of present-day Kent. Under the command of Aulus Plautius, the Romans won a battle against British tribes and advanced to the Thames. The river was much wider than it is today. Once it was crossed, the Romans established a protected settlement, which they called Londinium.

Right: Oil lamp in the shape of a foot, dating from the 2nd century.

Londinium the Capital

After 60 AD, Londinium was rebuilt as capital of the province. A system of roads was laid out by about the year 100. A hundred years later, Britain was divided into two provinces, and Londinium became capital of Upper Britain (York was capital of Lower Britain). During the 3rd century the city was generally peaceful and prosperous, but in the following century there was increasing pressure from northern tribes.

The Walled City

At first Londinium was surrounded by a bank and ditch. Around 200 a great wall was built around the city to the north of the Thames, from modern Blackfriars in the west to modern Tower Hill in the east. Made of ragstone, it was about 19 feet (6 m) high and 8 feet (2 m) thick at ground level. A riverside wall was added in the 4th century.

The forum and basilica stood in the middle of the walled city; the fort was at the northwest corner.

Public Buildings

Important buildings were made of ragstone and flat bricks. A new 547-feet (166 m) square forum was built around 120, on the highest ground to the east of the Walbrook. On its northern side was a basilica, which served as both a town hall and a law court. An amphitheater was built to the west of the city, and a fort served as a barracks for the troops.

Fort

Amphitheater

Forum and basilica

Temple of Mithras

Old London Bridge

River Thames

3rd-century pavement mosaic.

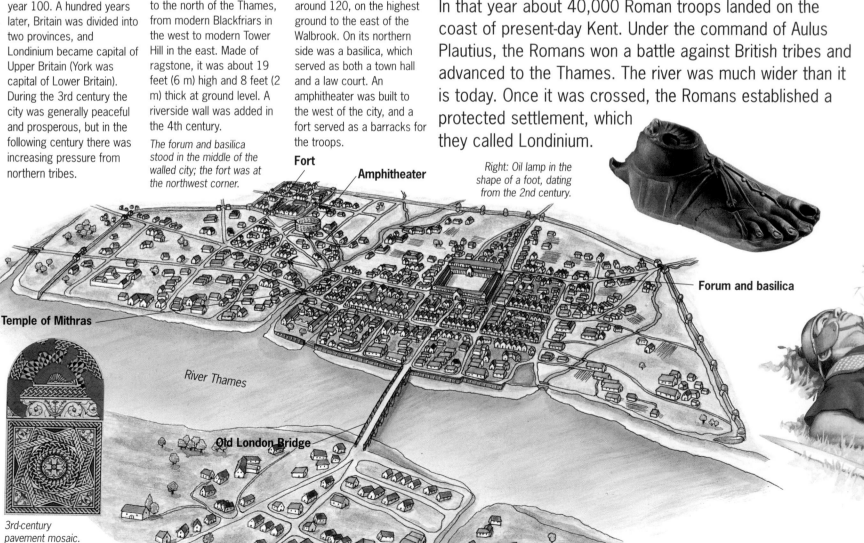

visits Britain for 16 days, receiving the surrender of 11 Celtic tribal rulers at Camulodunum (modern Colchester).

The Temple of Mithras

Mithras was an ancient Persian god of light, who was also worshiped in Rome. The temple dedicated to Mithras was built on the bank of the Walbrook stream, a tributary of the

Boudicca's Revolt

Boudicca was the widow of Prasutagus, ruler of a Celtic tribe in eastern Britain called the Iceni. On her husband's death, the Romans claimed the Iceni lands and treated Boudicca and her daughters badly. In 60 AD, under Boudicca's leadership, the Iceni and other tribes rebelled against Roman rule. The Britons sacked Londinium and burned it to

Boudicca leads an attack on the Romans. After her final defeat, in 62 AD, she took poison to avoid capture.

58 Military commander Suetonius Paulinus becomes governor of Roman Britain.

60 Prasutagus, ruler of the Celtic Iceni, dies.

c. 70 First Roman forum and wooden amphitheater built in Londinium.

71 Military commander

Left: Gold medallion showing Constantius Chlorus rescuing the city for the Romans.

Thames, around 240. It was a small building, just 59 feet (18 m) long and 26 feet (8 m) wide, with a nave, aisles, and a row of columns.

the ground. Suetonius Paulinus returned from Wales and routed the Britons. Emperor Nero then sent a new procurator to Britain, who in turn replaced Suetonius with a more understanding governor.

Cerialis becomes governor of Britain.

122 Emperor Hadrian (ruled 117–38) visits Londinium.

c. 125 Londinium is badly damaged by fire.

c. 200 First city walls built around Londinium.

Right: Marble statue of Mercury, found at the site of the Temple of Mithras.

286 Carausius declares himself emperor of Britain (he is murdered in 293).

c. 290 The Mint is established in Londinium.

296 Constantius Chlorus saves London from being sacked by rebels; he becomes Roman emperor in 305.

313 Emperor Constantine (ruled 312–37) makes Christianity legal throughout the empire.

314 A Christian bishop from Londinium attends the Council of Arles.

c. 350 Catapult towers added along the city walls.

Above: An artist's impression of the basilica in Roman times.

367 Hadrian's Wall is overrun.

368 Northern tribes threaten Londinium, but order is restored by military commander Theodosius.

410 Roman troops start leaving Londinium.

Trade

Trade was important to the growing port. Olives, figs, wine, bronze, and glass were imported from Rome. The main streets were full of shops, and the Roman historian Tacitus described the city as "famous for its crowd of traders and a great center of commerce." Timber quays were built in the 2nd century to help the loading and unloading of ships.

Below: Amphorae such as this were used for wine, olive oil, and fish sauce.

The Romans Leave

Following an increased number of raids by Picts and Scots from the north in the 4th century, in 410 Emperor Honorius decided to abandon his most northerly province. The Roman legions and administrators left

Stone relief of a Saxon warrior.

Londinium. This led to attacks from the European mainland, but life for most ordinary people of the city probably went on much the same.

446 – 1154

c. 446 Britons ask Rome for support against barbarian invaders.

597 Pope Gregory I sends St. Augustine with Christian missionaries to Britain.

604 A wooden church is founded and dedicated to St. Paul. Mellitus is appointed Bishop of London.

675–85 St. Paul's church is rebuilt in stone.

757–96 Reign of Offa, King of Mercia and overlord of the whole country (later called England, meaning "of the Angles").

842–51 Viking attacks on London and Canterbury.

c. 875 Alfred the Great campaigns and fights for London.

911 Edward the Elder (ruled 899–924) takes control of London.

962 St. Paul's minster is rebuilt after the Vikings loot and burn it.

994 Norwegian and Danish Vikings arrive in 94 ships and attack the city.

1013 Sweyn Forkbeard invades England with a large Danish force.

1016 Cnut (son of Forkbeard) captures London and becomes king of England.

1066–87 Reign of William I ("the Conqueror"), the first

Early Saxon London

After the Romans left, much of former Londinium lay in ruins and was largely deserted. Since they were from farming families, many of the Anglo-Saxon settlers were more interested in the fertile countryside than the former provincial capital. Nevertheless, by the end of the 6th century London was part of the kingdom of the East Saxons. Very little archeological evidence of early Saxon settlements has been found, but we know that the growing Saxon port was to the west of the old Roman city, along the present-day Strand.

Right: Saxon houses were wooden buildings, with sunken floors and pitched roofs of thatch or turf.

Saxon and Norman

Christianity Arrives

Pope Gregory I called on the head of a monastery in Rome to lead a band of missionaries to Britain. Augustine landed on the Isle of Thanet in 597 and was welcomed by Ethelbert, king of the Jutes in Kent. St. Augustine baptized the king (shown above) and converted thousands of his subjects to Christianity.

Alfred the Great

At the end of the 8th century, Vikings from Scandinavia began raiding towns in Britain. They eventually chose London as their winter quarters. In 886 Alfred (849–99), the Anglo-Saxon king of Wessex (the kingdom of the West Saxons), fought the invading Danes and won London back. Alfred refortified the old Roman city, making it a "burgh" and encouraging people to settle within the old city walls.

After the Romans left Londinium and their British province, the Celtic Britons were threatened with invasion from Picts and Scots. British chieftains were probably happy to see Germanic tribes from Jutland (in present-day Denmark) arrive. They thought the Jutes would help drive back the invaders, but the newcomers saw this as a great opportunity for establishing their own settlements. They were soon joined by more Germanic tribes — Angles and Saxons from present-day northern Germany. Saxons settled in and around London, which became a trading port known as Lundenwic. This attracted the attention of raiding Vikings, who were repelled before being replaced by conquering Normans.

Lundenwic

The growing Saxon settlement was called Lundenwic ("-wic" meaning port or trading town). Most of the Saxon settlers' trade was probably local, involving the buying and selling of farming produce. But there was also trade with other European river ports, and this may have concentrated on the famous British woolen cloth.

A 9th-century coin showing the head of Alfred the Great and the monogram Lvndonia (London).

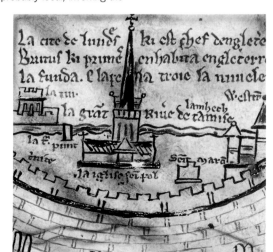

Above: Silver-gilt brooch found at an Anglo-Saxon burial site.

Urban Growth

Under the rule of Alfred and his successors, large parts of Lundenwic were developed. New streets were laid out in the center of the old Roman walled area, and many ruined Roman buildings, such as the amphitheater which survived into the medieval period, remained part of the city's landscape. A new bridge was constructed over the Thames, and quays were built along the riverside. By 1100, London had a population of over 10,000 and was steadily growing.

Left: The first known view of London was drawn by a monk around 1252.

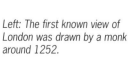

Norman king of England.

1068 William I's queen, Matilda, is crowned in Westminster Abbey.

1078 Building of the White Tower begins.

1097 National taxes are introduced to fund building projects in London.

Edward the Confessor

Edward was an Anglo-Saxon descended from Alfred, but he spent his youth in Normandy, in northwest France. He was crowned king of England in 1042 and made London his capital. Nicknamed "the Confessor"

1099 William II holds his first banquet in the new Westminster Hall.

1101 Rannulf de Flambard, Bishop of Durham, becomes the Tower of London's first prisoner (and later escapes).

1130–35 Henry I grants London a favorable charter.

for his piety, Edward built a new monastery dedicated to St. Peter in the west of flourishing London — the "west minster" (or Westminster), a church in the Norman style.

1136 The second wooden London Bridge is burnt down.

1147 Aldgate (the east gate of the Roman wall) is rebuilt.

1154 Death of the last Norman king, Stephen, who is succeeded by Plantagenet Henry II.

The Norman Conquest

On the death of Edward the Confessor, his cousin William, Duke of Normandy, claimed the throne. When Harold, Earl of Wessex, became king instead, William decided to invade. He

defeated Harold's troops at the Battle of Hastings and soon captured London. He was crowned William I of England on Christmas Day, 1066, in Westminster Abbey.

In 1086 William ordered a survey of English property holders, called the Domesday Book (above).

London

Famous Buildings

William I built a fortress so that he could control and protect London. Its south side was formed by the Thames, and the east by the Roman city wall. The first building within the fortress was a great keep called the White Tower. The fortress developed into the Tower of London. In the year of William's death (1087), work began on replacing the earlier church with a new Norman cathedral dedicated to St. Paul.

Old St. Paul's Cathedral was destroyed by fire in 1666.

Norman Rule

William II, son of William the Conqueror, was forced to put down a revolt by Norman barons, who wanted to increase their own power. His brother, Henry I (ruled 1100–35) strengthened his hold over the country.

Charters were drawn up giving citizens rights and protection in return for royal favor. But there were further troubles with nobles and religious leaders when Stephen, the last of the Norman kings, took the throne in 1135.

Above: Manuscripts such as this recorded London's customs and regulations.

Above: Edward the Confessor greets Harold, Earl of Wessex, in the royal hall at Westminster.

London Churches

Many large and wealthy monasteries, friaries, and nunneries were established in London in the 11th and 12th centuries. Old St. Paul's was the seat of the Bishop of London, who was a figure of national importance. Westminster Abbey was consecrated in 1065, and the crypt of St. Mary-le-Bow was built between 1070 and 1090 (using Roman bricks in its construction). The Church played an important part in shaping the appearance and character of medieval London.

This 13th-century crucifix was found at Bermondsey Priory, which was founded in 1082.

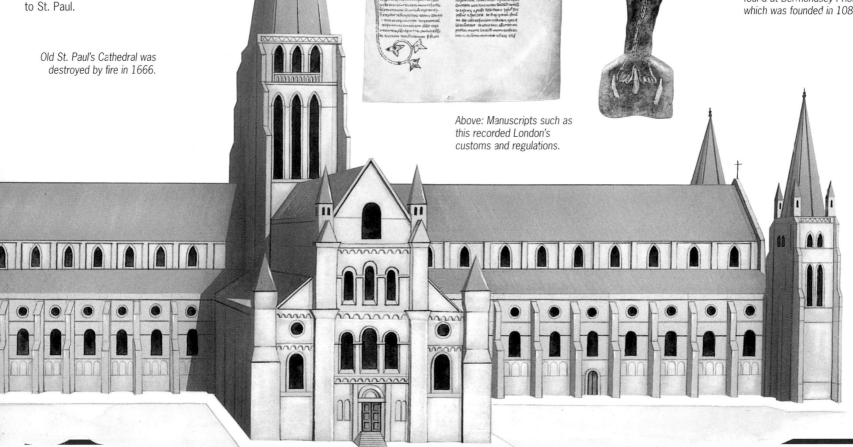

1154 – 1485

1154 First Plantagenet king, Henry II, is crowned in Westminster Abbey.

1158 The River Thames runs dry in London.

1189 Jews are banned from Richard the Lionheart's coronation.

Henry FitzAilwin is appointed London's first mayor.

1209 The first stone London Bridge is completed.

1224 England's chief

law courts are based at Westminster Hall.

1236 Lead pipes bring water to the City from Tyburn stream (off present Oxford Street).

1240 Old St. Paul's Cathedral is rededicated.

1246 A two-week annual fair is founded at Westminster by royal command.

1269 Unfinished Westminster Abbey is consecrated.

1274 The first town clerk is appointed in the city.

1283 The mayor of London is called "lord mayor" for the first time.

1326 Mobs riot and kill the bishop of Exeter at Cheapside.

Westminster

In medieval times, the manor of Westminster was separate from the City of London. It was dominated by Westminster Abbey, which was extensively rebuilt from the original church by Henry III (ruled 1216–72). During his reign, the first parliament was brought together in 1265 at Westminster Hall by Simon de Montfort (1208–65), the barons' leader. The Hall was part of the original Palace of Westminster, which was the main residence of English monarchs throughout the Middle Ages.

Above: Henry IV was crowned king in Westminster Abbey in 1399.

Everyday Life

Life for ordinary people was hard. The city's narrow streets were generally dirty and smelly, and there was a constant risk of wooden houses catching fire. In the 13th century thousands of Londoners died from famine. Then in 1348–49 a bubonic plague called the Black Death killed at least a third of the city's population.

These pots and jugs come from late 13th-century London.

Medieval London

During the Middle Ages London continued to be a busy trading port, and its center of commerce grew in importance. Medieval London was also the country's center of royalty and government, which was based at nearby Westminster. By the early 14th century there were probably around 80,000 people living in the city. Disease was rife, however, and when the Black Death struck in 1348, the city's population was dramatically reduced. A mayor headed a governing city council, and in return for their civic oath and a donation of taxes, citizens had the right to trade, buy and sell property, and benefit from the city's courts. Most Londoners were not full citizens, however, and earned their living as unskilled laborers.

Merchants used small handheld scales like these for weighing coins and metal, to determine their value.

Merchants and Trade

By 1180 there were already many guilds (or merchants' associations) in London, including those of cloth workers, butchers, and goldsmiths. Wool and cloth were the main export goods, along with Cornish tin. As England's main port, London was also an important marketplace for imported goods and luxury wares, such as spices, furs, and wine. This encouraged many foreign merchants, especially from Flanders and Italy, to move to London.

The Peasants' Revolt

In 1381 English peasants rebelled against high taxes and forced labor. Led by a man called Wat Tyler, they marched to London. Many were killed in the riots, including merchants and lawyers. King Richard II (ruled 1377–99), who was just 14 years old, met Tyler and others at Smithfield. Tyler was killed and the rebellion ended.

The Tower of London

The Tower's south side was formed by the River Thames, and its east side by the old Roman wall. William the Conqueror's fortress continued to be used by Plantagenet kings to control and protect London. It became customary for a new king to stay in the Tower before his coronation.

Above: An early illustration of the Tower. In the foreground is Traitors' Gate, through which prisoners were brought by boat. Further up the Thames, beyond the White Tower, is London Bridge.

Other residents were less fortunate: they were held prisoner in the Tower before being executed on Tower Hill.

Believing the king to be under threat, mayor William Walworth killed Wat Tyler.

1329 Thames fishermen are fined for using nets with too small holes.

1340 Poet Geoffrey Chaucer is born, probably at his parents' house in Upper Thames Street.

1348 The Black Death strikes London and kills thousands.

1397 Dick Whittington (later an English folk hero) becomes mayor.

1403 The Priory of St. Mary Bethlehem opens a hospital for "distracted" patients, later known as Bedlam.

1411 Rebuilding of the Guildhall begins.

1461 Edward IV knights many London citizens for their support in the Wars of the Roses.

1476 William Caxton sets up a printing press at Westminster.

1483 Murder of the princes Edward and Richard (Edward IV's sons) in the Tower of London.

1485 Richard III, last king of the House of York, is killed at Bosworth Field.

Royal Charter

Just weeks before he approved the famous Magna Carta, King John (reigned 1199–1216) confirmed London's right to govern itself. After having great problems with his barons, John agreed to a charter giving London's citizens the right to elect their own mayor.

Left: The royal charter of King John was drawn up in 1215.

London Bridge

A wooden bridge across the Thames had stood since Roman times, but it was destroyed in 1014 in order to divide invading Danish forces. This event was the origin of the nursery rhyme, "London Bridge is falling down." The bridge was later rebuilt in wood, and the first stone bridge across the Thames was completed in 1209. It was built on piers made of wooden stakes driven into the riverbed and filled with rubble. These supported 19 stone arches, with a drawbridge at the southern end. The bridge was crowded with houses and shops, up to seven storeys high, on both sides. These included a chapel dedicated to St. Thomas Becket. The carriageway between the buildings was less than 13 feet (4 m) wide, so pedestrians, carts, and animals made slow progress. There was a towered gateway, where it soon became the gruesome custom to display the heads of traitors on spikes.

Busy markets, such as this one beside London Bridge, were common in medieval London. Boats full of produce could moor at wharves near the bridge.

King Henry VIII (reigned 1509–47) ended the authority of the pope in England so that he could obtain a divorce.

Church and Government

In 1533 Parliament declared that England was independent of the pope. The following year, at the insistence of Henry VIII, further acts completed England's break with the Roman Catholic Church. The

Monastic Property

When Henry VIII dissolved monasteries and suppressed monastic houses, the property was transferred to the Crown and created great wealth. Local landowners, favored courtiers, and government officials all benefited. In some areas of London, more than half of the property had previously been owned by the Church. There were 12 monasteries, including the Benedictine

Church of England became a separate institution, and the king was its supreme head. This led to the policy of dissolving monasteries, which changed the face of London.

Right: Rosary and prayer book of Queen Mary I (reigned 1553–58), who was a devout Catholic.

Westminster Abbey, 25 hospitals belonging to religious orders, several nunneries, and many houses belonging to friars and canons. All were confiscated, and some were vandalized. The Franciscan Greyfriars monastery, in Newgate Street, was used as a store for wine and fish.

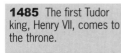
1485 – 1714

1485 The first Tudor king, Henry VII, comes to the throne.

1513 Dockyards are built at Woolwich and Deptford.

1536 Anne Boleyn (Henry VIII's second wife) is beheaded on

Tower Green.

1540 Westminster Abbey is surrendered to the king's agents by the abbot and 24 monks.

1576 London's first theater opens in Shoreditch.

1600 Founding of the

Above: Portrait medal of Elizabeth I (reigned 1558–1603), the daughter of Henry VIII and his second wife, Anne Boleyn, who was executed at the Tower of London in 1536.

The Civil War

The first Stuart king, James I (reigned 1603–25) believed in the "divine right of kings." He tried to rule as an absolute monarch, but Parliament did not allow this. His son, Charles I (reigned 1625–49), continued the

Tudor and

During this period the growth of London's population was once again checked by terrible outbreaks of plague. Nevertheless, by 1600 there were around 200,000 Londoners, and in the 17th century the numbers went on increasing rapidly. Commerce and art both flourished in England's capital, especially during the Elizabethan period of 1558 to 1603. During the Civil War, Londoners supported Parliament against the monarchy, but this changed dramatically during the Restoration period. After the Great Fire of London in 1666, large parts of the city were rebuilt, and a period of expansion began.

The Restoration

Two years after Cromwell's death, Parliament restored the monarchy and named Charles II (son of Charles I) king. This new period of Stuart rule is known as the Restoration. Londoners welcomed their new king, and the more relaxed atmosphere that existed under his rule. Court life at St. James' and Whitehall palaces was livelier again, and Charles even wanted to build a new palace at Greenwich, but he lacked the money to complete it. Then two great disasters struck London — plague and fire.

Remembering the Great Plague of 1665: a book which recorded deaths, an iron bell to announce the collection of the dead, and a commemorative plate and spoon.

Above: Samuel Pepys wrote about life in Charles II's London.

Samuel Pepys

The diarist Samuel Pepys (1633–1706) is most widely known for his *Diary*, in which he provides vivid details of the social life of London's upper-classes during the Restoration period. He also described the devastation caused in London by the plague and the Great Fire.

In 1605 Guy Fawkes (shown second from right, with other Catholic conspirators) hid barrels of gunpowder in a cellar beneath the Palace of Westminster. However, their plot to blow up Parliament was discovered, and Fawkes was executed.

Right: View of London from the south, painted by an artist of the Dutch School around 1630.

East India Company.

1603 The first Stuart king, James I (James VI of Scotland), enters London through Aldersgate on his way to Whitehall and the Tower.

1613 The New River supplies water to London through wooden pipes.

1622 The new Banqueting House in Whitehall, designed by Inigo Jones, is completed.

1631 Inigo Jones designs Covent Garden.

1637 Hyde Park is opened to the public.

1642 Trenches and ramparts are built around the city for protection with the outbreak of the Civil War.

1652 The first coffee house opens in London.

1660 The Royal Society (for the Advancement of Natural Science) is founded at

Gresham College in Broad Street. Daniel Defoe (author of *Robinson Crusoe*) is born in Fore Street.

1665 The Great Plague kills more than 80,000 Londoners.

1675 The Royal Observatory is founded at Greenwich.

1681 The Royal Hospital at Chelsea is founded.

1682 Downing Street is built as a cul-de-sac of terraced brick houses.

1688 The so-called "Glorious Revolution" brings the reign of James II to an end.

1697 The first service is held in Wren's rebuilt St. Paul's Cathedral.

1701 Pirate Captain Kidd is hanged at Execution Dock, Wapping.

1714 The last Stuart monarch, Queen Anne, dies at Kensington Palace.

quest for total power and finally dissolved Parliament. The Civil War (1642–51) broke out, and London became a center of anti-royalist and pro-Parliament Roundheads. Their forces finally won the day, and in 1649 Charles I was beheaded outside the

Banqueting House in Whitehall. England became a republic, and power was taken by a leading general, Oliver Cromwell.

Above: The royal standard of Charles I.

Left: Bust of Oliver Cromwell (1599–1658), who took the title Lord Protector.

Stuart London

Trade and Commerce

Companies of merchants helped increase London's influence on the international market. This was still mainly based on the export of cloth. Their success meant that Londoners' wages were higher than those of provincial workers. A Royal

From the 1650s, business was often conducted in coffee houses such as this.

Exchange was opened by Elizabeth I in 1571, and this quickly became a great international trading center. The Bank of England was founded over a hundred years later, in 1694.

Below: The stone Monument was designed by Sir Christopher Wren and completed in 1677. It was built to commemorate the Great Fire and stands 202 feet (61.5 m) high, the same distance to the west of Pudding Lane, where the fire broke out.

The Great Fire

Early in the morning of September 2, 1666, fire broke out in a baker's shop in Pudding Lane, near London Bridge. Fires were not uncommon, but this time winds spread the flames quickly and Londoners were helpless. The city burned for five days, and within the old walls about three quarters of

the buildings were destroyed. St. Paul's Cathedral was burned down, along with 87 churches, the Guildhall, the Royal Exchange, and more than 13,000 houses. Amazingly, few people were killed.

Below: The Great Fire of London swept through the city.

Housing

Before the Great Fire, most London houses were timber-framed, with a few made of stone. After 1666, the area within the walls had to be rebuilt, and most new houses were made of brick. Streets were widened and obstructions removed, reducing the danger of fire, though many older timber houses still remained. Acts were passed to introduce building standards for different types of houses.

Below: This pre-fire Tudor house stood in Cornhill, the highest hill in the city and site of the Roman basilica. It was owned by the Clothworkers' Company.

Dickens

Charles Dickens (1812–70), moved with his family to London when he was about two years old. After working as a boy in a boot-polish factory, Dickens began writing about the hardships of working-class life in Victorian England. His gripping stories were serialized in weekly magazines and over the years became best-sellers.

Left: A scene from Oliver!, the 1968 film of Dickens' novel Oliver Twist, set in a London poorhouse. The film won six Oscars.

Above: The Canterbury Tales. Chaucer's pilgrims traveled from London to Canterbury, telling tales on the way.

ART, LITERATURE, AND THEATER

1400 Geoffrey Chaucer is buried in Westminster Abbey (the first in Poets' Corner).

c.1567 The Old Curiosity Shop (probably the inspiration for Dickens' novel) opens in Portsmouth Street.

c.1588 William Shakespeare moves from

Chaucer

The famous English poet Geoffrey Chaucer was born in London around 1340, probably in his parents' house in Upper Thames Street. Chaucer's father was a well-off wine merchant and innkeeper. Geoffrey spent much of his life in London, and set the opening of his most famous work, *The Canterbury Tales*, at the Tabard Inn in Southwark.

Virginia Woolf (1882–1941) lived in Gordon Square in London and was a central figure in the Bloomsbury group. Her novels include Mrs Dalloway (1925) and Orlando (1928).

Art, Literature,

Geoffrey Chaucer, John Donne, John Milton, William Turner, Dante Gabriel Rossetti, Virginia Woolf, Harold Pinter … these are just some of the famous and successful writers, dramatists, painters, and poets who were born and brought up in London. Many others have lived and worked in the city during their productive years, including William Shakespeare and Charles Dickens. The talents of these individuals have enriched the city immensely. At the same time, London's great theaters, museums, galleries, libraries, and academies have helped build its cultural traditions and continue to foster its artistic vitality.

The Bloomsbury Group

The entrance to Tate Britain on Millbank.

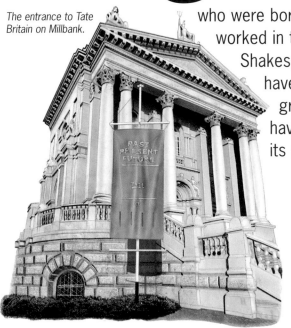

The Bloomsbury group was the name given to a circle of English writers, artists, and philosophers who met in the Bloomsbury area of London in the early 20th century. The "Bloomsberries," as they were known, discussed philosophical questions and shared their ideas on life. Its members included artists Vanessa Bell and Duncan Grant, the novelists E.M. Forster and Virginia Woolf, and others such as Clive Bell and John Maynard Keynes.

London Characters

According to Arthur Conan Doyle's stories, Sherlock Holmes (right) and his partner, Dr. Watson lived in London from 1881–1904.

Sir Arthur Conan Doyle's fictional detective *Sherlock Holmes* began solving cases from 221b Baker Street in 1887. J.M. Barrie's play *Peter Pan* was first staged in London in 1904, and parts were published as a novel called *Peter Pan in Kensington Gardens*. A.A. Milne's *Winnie-the-Pooh* (1926) was named after a real black bear in London Zoo, while P.L.Travers' *Mary Poppins* stories about a magical nanny first appeared in 1934, and were made into a popular Disney film 30 years later.

Tate Britain

The original Tate Gallery was opened in 1897, changing its name to Tate Britain when its collection of international modern art was transferred to the new Tate Modern at Bankside in 2000. Tate Britain exhibits a wide collection of British art from the 16th to the 21st centuries, with a special gallery devoted to works by the landscape painter William Turner, which the artist left to the nation on his death in 1851.

The Royal Academy

The Royal Academy of Arts was founded in 1768, with the famous portrait and landscape painter Thomas Gainsborough among its founding members. The Academy, based in the Palladian splendor of Burlington House in Piccadilly, holds exhibitions as well as conducting art schools. John Constable, along with the leading members of the Pre-Raphaelite Brotherhood — William Holman Hunt, John Everett Millais, and Dante Gabriel Rossetti — were all students at the Academy. It continues to hold its famous summer exhibition, which has been running for more than 200 years.

La Ghirlandata (1873) by Dante Gabriel Rossetti (1828–82).

Stratford to London.

1613 Shakespeare's Globe Theatre burns down.

1623 A "music house" is built by Thomas Sadler beside a well, becoming Sadler's Wells Theatre.

1774 Thomas Gainsborough (1727–88)

moves to London.

1818 The Old Vic Theatre opens as a "house of melodrama."

1824 The National Gallery is founded.

1839 Charles Dickens completes *Oliver Twist*.

1848 The Pre-Raphaelite Brotherhood is founded.

1890 William Morris founds the Kelmscott Press in Hammersmith.

1912 A statue of Peter Pan is put up in Kensington Gardens.

1947 The Institute of Contemporary Arts is founded.

1956 John Osborne's *Look Back in Anger* is staged at the Royal Court Theatre.

1958 Harold Pinter's *The Birthday Party* is staged at the Lyric, Hammersmith. The National Film Theatre opens

on the South Bank.

1962 Laurence Olivier is appointed director of the National Theatre.

1970 The Young Vic Theatre opens.

1985 The Saatchi Gallery of contemporary art opens.

1996 New replica of the

Globe Theatre opens.

1999 Renovated Royal Opera House reopens in Covent Garden.

2003 The Andrew Lloyd Webber Collection goes on show at the Royal Academy.

Shakespeare

William Shakespeare (1564–1616) (right) was a brilliant playwright, poet, and actor. He is considered by many experts to be the greatest dramatist who ever lived. Much of his best work was done in London, where

the theater was very popular with all classes of society. Shakespeare was seen as a practical dramatist rather than a literary writer, and he became the city's most popular playwright. Around 1610 he retired from the London stage and returned to his native Stratford.

Underground Poetry

Since 1986, poems have been displayed on posters on Tube trains, platforms, and escalators, helping to brighten up Londoners' Underground journeys. The poems have proved so popular that selections have

also been published as books (see above).

Above: George Bernard Shaw wrote Pygmalion, *about a Cockney flower girl, in 1913. It was later turned into a hit musical,* My Fair Lady.

and Theater

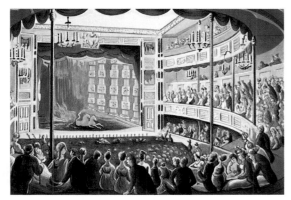

A performance at Sadler's Wells Theatre in 1809. Today the theater presents works by international modern-dance companies.

Musicals

In 1881 the Savoy Theatre in the Strand opened for the production of comic operas written and composed by

William Gilbert and Arthur Sullivan. Gilbert and Sullivan's works, such as *The Pirates of Penzance*, were hugely successful. In recent years, Sir Andrew Lloyd Webber (born in London in 1948) has had a string of enormously popular musicals produced on the London stage, including *Jesus Christ Superstar*, *Evita*, *Cats* (based on poems by London resident T.S. Eliot) and *Starlight Express*.

Right: Cast members of Cats, *which ran for a record 21 years on the West End stage.*

Playwrights

Two Irish dramatists had a great influence on London theater. Oscar Wilde (1854–1900) settled in Chelsea and delighted audiences with comedies such as *The Importance of Being Earnest* (1895), which was first staged at St. James's Theatre. George Bernard Shaw (1856–1950) moved to London at the age of 20, and in 1884 joined the socialist Fabian Society. His early works were unpopular, but he made his name with innovative plays such as *Man and Superman* (1905), which were put on at the progressive Royal Court Theatre.

Below: A Private View at the Royal Academy (1881) by William Powell Frith.

1714 – 1830

1714 George Louis of Brunswick-Lüneberg becomes George I, the first Hanoverian king of Great Britain.

1722 Carriages are ordered to drive on the left crossing London Bridge, and the rule soon spreads to all streets.

1740 London Hospital is founded. Bow Street magistrates' court is established.

1758–62 The houses are removed from London Bridge.

1759 The British Museum is opened to the public.

1762 George III buys Buckingham House (later rebuilt as Buckingham Palace).

1764 House numbering begins (probably in New Burlington Street).

1766 The city wall is demolished.

1770s Fortnum and Mason grocery shop opens in Piccadilly.

1787 The first county match (between Middlesex and Essex) is played at Lord's cricket ground in St. John's Wood.

1797 Hatchard's bookshop opens at No.

173 Piccadilly.

1798 Founding of the River Police at the Port of London.

1801 First census shows 959,310 people in London, and 1,096,784 in Greater London.

1802 After studying at

Urban Development

The area covered by London more than doubled during the 18th century. Urban landowners became more prosperous, while those who had made fortunes from commercial ventures lived in fine houses in elegant residential areas such as Mayfair. There the wide streets had good sidewalks and the houses were set well back. At the same time, many middle-class Londoners moved away from the City and the East End, and separate business districts developed. For the less wealthy, housing problems increased, and high rents were charged for poor accommodation.

Transportation

Wealthy Londoners had their own horses and stables for their private carriages, and one-seater sedan chairs were also carried by strong footmen. Hackney carriages had been introduced in the 17th century, and by 1770 there were a thousand licensed coachmen in London. Licensed watermen worked their way up and down the Thames and ferried people across the river.

Carts and carriages jostle for space along Cornhill.

Above: Grosvenor Square, in Mayfair in about 1754. This part of town attracted very wealthy residents.

Downing Street

No. 10 Downing Street was acquired by the Crown in 1732. George II offered the house as a personal gift to Robert Walpole, who was First Lord of the Treasury, and he accepted it in the name of his office. The

Below: A bustling scene at the Covent Garden market in the early 18th century.

Right: Robert Walpole is regarded as having been Britain's first prime minister from 1721 to 1742, though the title was not used at the time.

property was renovated and decorated by William Kent, and Walpole lived there occasionally. Since then No. 10 has been the official residence of the prime minister, though many have preferred to remain in their own town houses.

Georgian London

The four Hanoverian Georges ruled Britain from 1714 to 1830, and during this period London continued to be the hub of the country. Wealthy Londoners wanted substantial houses in the West End, and soon Mayfair and Piccadilly were full of fashionable squares and streets. Many were designed by great architects such as Robert Adam and John Nash. However, there was also great squalor, and many Londoners lived in highly unsanitary conditions with no clean water or sewers. By 1800 conditions had improved, and the city was much bigger and more stylish. By then there were about a million Londoners, making it the largest city in the world.

the Royal Academy, John Constable exhibits his first paintings there. The Stock Exchange is given new premises in Capel Court.

1807 Gas lighting is demonstrated in Pall Mall to mark the Prince of Wales' birthday.

1812 John Bellingham, assassin of Prime Minister Spencer Percival, is hanged at Newgate Prison.

1813 Fog covers London for seven days.

1820 Regent's Canal, from Paddington to the Thames at Limehouse, is opened.

1826 The Zoological Society of London is founded; London Zoo opens two years later.

1829 London's Metropolitan Police force is founded; policemen are nicknamed "Peelers" after home secretary Sir Robert Peel. The first horse bus is seen on London's streets.

1830 An era ends as George IV dies.

Kings and Ministers

George I (reigned 1714–27), a great-grandson of James I, became king when his distant cousin Queen Anne died. Since he knew little of British politics and spoke no English, he turned to his ministers, especially the influential Robert Walpole. The king's son, George II (reigned 1727–60), also relied on Walpole. In 1743, he became the last British king to appear in battle, against the French. His grandson, who became George III (reigned 1760–1820), suffered from poor mental health in later life. He was succeeded by his son, who became regent in 1811 and king nine years later.

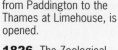

Left: George III is mainly remembered as the "mad king" who lost Britain its American colonies.

Above: Front page of the first issue of The Times, dated January 1, 1788. It had been launched three years earlier as the Daily Universal Register. Its owner promised that the new four-page newspaper would not support any particular political party.

Everyday Life

Sanitation generally improved during the 18th century, and many waterwork companies opened after 1760. Street lighting was developed, and by the end of the period some gaslights had been introduced. Dirty, dangerous industries were forced to move outside the boundaries of the city, and there were more open public spaces. Nevertheless, many people came to London without work or accommodation, and poor people were taken off the streets and put in workhouses. There they were given basic food and shelter in return for unpaid work.

Georgian streets were busy and very noisy. The artist William Hogarth (1697–1764) painted the misery and immorality of London's streets during the 18th century. The names of some of his paintings — Gin Lane and Beer Street for example — tell us of the problem of alcoholism among the London poor.

Left: This brocaded silk dress was woven in London around 1750.

Chippendale chair from 1760.

Art and Culture

In addition to military matters, George II's other great interest was music. The king loved opera and was a generous patron of the German-born composer George Frederick Handel (1685–1759) who had moved to London in 1712, and lived for more than 30 years in Brook Street, near Hanover Square. Handel wrote for the Royal Opera House at Covent Garden, which opened in 1732. Six years later he became a founding member of the Royal Society of Musicians in London. Many other museums, galleries, and cultural societies opened in London in the 18th century.

Along the Thames

For centuries there had been ferries across the Thames, and its banks were lined with steps where passengers could embark. But London needed more bridges, and in 1729 the new wooden Fulham Bridge opened (later called Putney Bridge). Then in 1750 the long-awaited stone bridge at Westminster was finished, and this was soon followed by Blackfriars Bridge. Architects such as the Adam brothers also designed imposing riverside developments. The Adelphi project included an elegant row of terraced buildings, which had apartments above and warehouses below, with a series of archways from which goods could be collected by barge.

In 1774 the Royal Society of Arts moved to an imposing building (left) that was then part of the Adam brothers' Adelphi scheme. Today it is in John Adam Street.

Below: Westminster Bridge in 1749.

Georgian Style

Georgian architects followed the principles of classical Greek and Roman buildings, especially as revived by the 16th-century Italian architect Palladio (see page 29). Later, during the regency and reign of George IV (reigned 1820–30), they developed styles known as Gothic Revival and Regency. George IV employed John Nash (1752–1835) to redevelop parts of London. Nash laid out the terraces around Regent's Park, as well as Regent Street, linking the park to Pall Mall. In interior design, wallpaper replaced wood paneling, and Thomas Chippendale (1718–79) designed and made famous Georgian furniture. In dress, the fashion was for elaborate designs for both men and women.

Right: This design for a London town house dates from 1774.

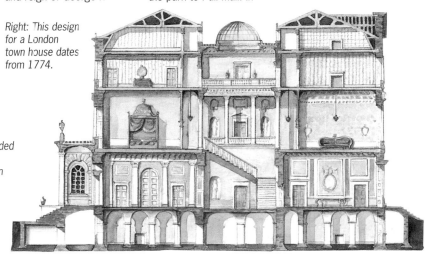

1837 – 1901

1837 Victoria becomes queen of the United Kingdom on the death of her uncle, William IV (who reigned from 1830).

1840 Queen Victoria marries her first cousin, Albert in the Chapel Royal of St. James's Palace.

1843 Nelson's Column is completed in Trafalgar Square.

1844 Pentonville prison has its first inmates.

1845 The first University Boat Race (Oxford v. Cambridge) is rowed on the Thames from Putney to Mortlake.

1849 Henry Charles Harrod opens a grocer's shop in Knightsbridge, founding Harrods.

1852 The Crystal Palace is removed from Hyde Park and rebuilt at Sydenham, in Kent.

1863 Opening of the world's first underground railway, the Metropolitan, from Paddington to Farringdon Road.

1866 The Metropolitan Fire Brigade is formed.

1871 The Royal Albert Hall is completed.

1878 Electric lights are installed along the Embankment beside the Thames.

1881 The Natural History Museum opens in Cromwell Road.

1884 The first public lavatory for ladies opens at Oxford Circus.

1886 The Arsenal Football

Transportation

London's first main-line railroad terminus, Euston, opened in the year that Victoria became queen. It was followed in 1838 by Paddington station, and rail links throughout London and to other cities grew rapidly (see page 27). Horse-drawn omnibuses (stagecoaches) also operated throughout London, and by the 1880s they were joined on the busy roads by two- and three-wheel cycles. At the end of the 19th century, however, the roads were still crowded with all sorts of horse-drawn carts and carriages.

Above: Building the Thames Tunnel beneath the river between Wapping and Rotherhithe. The tunnel opened in 1843 for pedestrians, and was converted for the East London Railway in the 1860s.

Victorian streets were full of life. Much of today's London still reflects Victorian building.

After the Houses of Parliament were destroyed by fire in 1834, they were rebuilt and the new House of Commons opened in 1852. Seven years later, the Big Ben bell and clock tower (left) came into operation.

Right: The world's first postage stamp, the "Penny Black," was issued in 1840.

POSTAGE
ONE PENNY

Urban Development

In early Victorian times the standards of water and sanitation were very poor. Workers' houses were overcrowded. But things improved when well-meaning businessmen put money into better housing for working families, and almshouses were built for some poor, elderly, and infirm Londoners. During the 1860s a vast system of underground sewers was built, and when this was completed in 1875, it had a great effect on ordinary Londoners' health and quality of life.

Middle-Class Style

The London middle classes lived in comfortable homes. There was a coal fireplace in most rooms (leading to smoke pollution throughout the city), and families had time for leisure in the drawing room. Many households had a cook, a parlor maid, and a housemaid, and even some working-class families employed a young relative as a maid. Large households had their own laundry maid.

Club is formed as Dial Square, changing its name to Woolwich Arsenal in 1891.

1888 The Whitechapel murders are committed by the infamous "Jack the Ripper."

1889 London County Council is established. The Savoy Hotel opens in the Strand.

Queen Victoria

Alexandrina Victoria was born at Kensington Palace, London, in 1819. She was the only child of Edward, the son of King George III, and Victoria Maria Louisa, the daughter of a German duke. She became queen in 1837, and three years later

1892 William Morris opens the Kelmscott Press in Hammersmith.

1894 The Tower Bridge is opened by the Prince of Wales.

1897 The Tate Gallery opens (sponsored by Sir Henry Tate, the sugar refiner). The first motorbus

married Albert, a German prince. They had nine children before Albert died in 1861. Victoria was proclaimed Empress of India in 1876, as the British Empire increased in size, power, and wealth. She ruled for nearly 64 years, longer than any other British monarch.

is licensed in London.

1898 The city's first escalator is installed in Harrods.

1901 Queen Victoria dies and is succeeded by her eldest son, Edward VII.

Victoria was crowned in Westminster Abbey in 1838. The present Imperial State Crown (right), kept with the Crown Jewels at the Tower of London, is very similar to the one used at Victoria's coronation.

Health and Education

Serious diseases included typhus, diphtheria, and tuberculosis. In 1859 a cholera epidemic swept through London, killing 13,000 people. Most ordinary Londoners could not afford to visit a doctor, because they had to pay for his services, and

hospitals could scarcely cope. In 1870 schools were set up for 5 to 10 year olds, but they were not free and the children of poor families stayed away. Some went to "ragged schools" run by churches and charities.

Below: A poor woman and baby around 1877.

Victorian London

The Great Exhibition

In 1851 London and Britain both celebrated their important global role by holding the first great

world's fair. The Great Exhibition, which was very much the idea of Prince Albert (1819–61), was held in Hyde Park. The main building was a giant greenhouse

called the Crystal Palace, where over 100,000 industrial exhibits were shown. More than half the 14,000 exhibitors were British, and the emphasis was on Britain and its capital being the "workshop of the world." The 20-week event was a great success.

During the long reign of Queen Victoria, London was a city of great contrasts. It was at the heart of a successful empire and became the financial capital of the world. The Great Exhibition celebrated this very fact, and showed the world the industrial and technological progress Britain had made. At the same time, there was enormous development in the city, as the middle classes expanded and former green spaces between districts filled with streets. Yet there was also terrible poverty and urban decay, as many thousands moved to London but failed to find work or affordable housing. A third of Londoners were still living below the poverty line by the 1890s, when the total population was approaching six million.

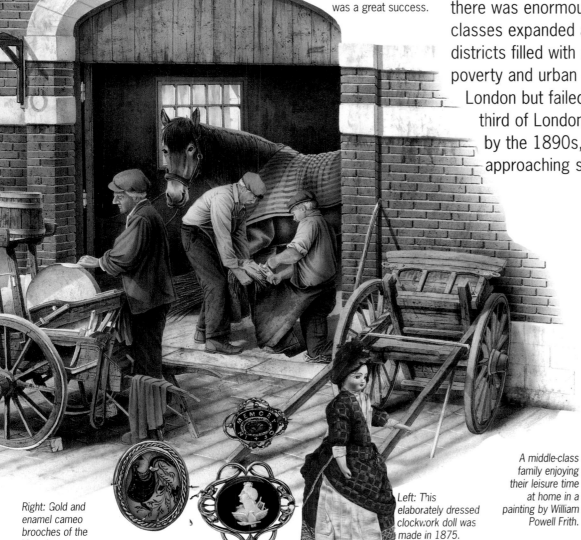

Right: Gold and enamel cameo brooches of the Victorian era.

Left: This elaborately dressed clockwork doll was made in 1875.

Season ticket to the exhibition, with a souvenir box showing the Crystal Palace.

A middle-class family enjoying their leisure time at home in a painting by William Powell Frith.

886 London comes under the rule of Alfred the Great.

1066 William the Conqueror is crowned in Westminster Abbey on Christmas Day.

1303 Treasure is stolen from the Royal Treasury in Westminster Abbey; the Keeper of the Royal Palace is hanged for the theft.

1399 The City and Parliament depose Richard II.

1554 Princess Elizabeth (later Queen) is held in the Tower for two months.

1637 Charles I encloses Richmond Park as a hunting ground.

1661 New Crown Jewels are made for the coronation of Charles II.

1689 The royal court moves to St. James's Palace.

1698 Whitehall Palace is destroyed by fire.

1759 Augusta, Dowager Princess of Wales, establishes the Royal Botanic Gardens at Kew.

1825 The Royal Mews (stables and coach houses designed by John Nash) is completed.

1847 Buckingham Palace is completed.

1850 The East India Company presents Queen Victoria with the legendary diamond, the "Koh-i-noor."

1880 The first Royal Tournament is held in Islington.

1911 The Mall (created 1660) is widened to form a processional approach to

Royal London

London has been a royal city for almost a thousand years. The sovereigns of England, and later the United Kingdom, have always lived in the capital and run their affairs of state from there. The present Queen lives in Buckingham Palace, and there are many other royal buildings, parks, and monuments throughout the city. Traditional royal ceremonies, such as Trooping the Color and the State Opening of Parliament, as well as weddings and funerals, continue to be held in London. Probably the most famous royal building in the city is Buckingham Palace, which has hosted some of city's most magnificent celebrations, including those for Elizabeth II's Golden Jubilee.

capital of his realm. Since 1066, every coronation has taken place in Westminster Abbey. In 1396 Richard II had his portrait (below) placed in the Abbey, to remind his people that his authority came from God. The painting still hangs on a column of the south aisle. In 1838 Queen Victoria had a splendid coronation procession, accompanied by firework displays in Hyde Park and Green Park. Elizabeth II continued the tradition, being crowned in Westminster Abbey (see page 35) and living in Buckingham Palace.

Kings and Queens

Edward the Confessor (reigned 1042–66) began the tradition of making London the royal center and

Above: Portrait of Richard II, who was crowned in London at the age of ten.

Modern Royalty

Many of London's traditional ceremonies and customs involve the Queen or other members of the royal family. The monarch is the United Kingdom's Head of State, and the political party that wins a general election officially forms Her Majesty's government. The prime minister has regular

Above: Elizabeth II celebrated her Golden Jubilee (50 years on the throne) in 2002. She rode to St. Paul's Cathedral in the Gold State Coach.

meetings with the Queen at Buckingham Palace, where she lives for much of the year. When the Queen is in residence, the Royal Standard is flown at the palace's masthead.

Monuments

There are many famous royal monuments in London. Charing Cross was originally the last of twelve crosses put up by Edward I to mark his wife's funeral route to Westminster Abbey in 1290. A 19th-century replica stands in Charing Cross station. The Albert Memorial, in Kensington Gardens, was

put up in 1876 as a memorial to Queen Victoria's husband. In 1998 the regilded statue was unveiled by Queen Elizabeth II.

Right: The Queen Victoria Memorial, outside Buckingham Palace, was unveiled by George V in 1911. The marble statue of the queen is seated beneath a gold-leafed figure of Victory.

Buckingham Palace.

1953 Queen Elizabeth II is crowned in Westminster Abbey.

1962 The Queen's Gallery opens to hold exhibitions of art from the royal collection.

1981 Charles, Prince of Wales, marries Lady Diana

Spencer in St. Paul's Cathedral.

1997 Funeral procession and service in Westminster Abbey for Diana, Princess of Wales.

2002 Funeral procession and service in Westminster Abbey for Queen Elizabeth, the Queen Mother.

Palaces

Below: King George V (reigned 1910–36) and Queen Mary attending a thanksgiving service at Westminster Abbey in 1935. In the foreground are Yeomen of the Guard, personal bodyguards of the British sovereign since the reign of Henry VII. They continue to wear Tudor costume.

Queen Victoria was the first monarch to live in Buckingham Palace, and it has been a royal residence ever since. Several other London palaces and mansions act as official homes for the royal family. Clarence House, overlooking the Mall, was

the home of Queen Elizabeth, the Queen Mother until her death in 2002. It is now the official residence of the heir to the throne, Prince Charles. Both Kensington and St. James's Palaces house the offices and personal apartments of other members of the royal family.

Above: View of Buckingham Palace from the Mall. Some rooms are open to the public in summer.

Right: Members of the royal family on the balcony at Buckingham Palace in 1991.

Below: The Irish State Coach, made in Dublin in 1852, was bought by Queen Victoria for riding to the State Opening of Parliament. It is still used for the royal procession.

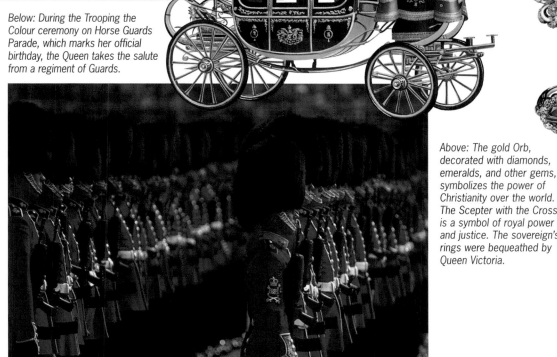

Ceremonies

For the annual State Opening of Parliament, there is a royal procession from Buckingham Palace to the Houses of Parliament. The ceremony in the House of Lords is not open to the public, but nowadays is televised. Trooping the Color is also an annual event, while the ceremony of Changing the Guard at Buckingham Palace normally takes place every day from April to July. The Queen's Guards are changed even when she is not in residence.

Below: St. James's Park in 1794.

Below: During the Trooping the Colour ceremony on Horse Guards Parade, which marks her official birthday, the Queen takes the salute from a regiment of Guards.

Above: The gold Orb, decorated with diamonds, emeralds, and other gems, symbolizes the power of Christianity over the world. The Scepter with the Cross is a symbol of royal power and justice. The sovereign's rings were bequeathed by Queen Victoria.

Crown Jewels

The treasured regalia of the sovereigns of England, known as the Crown Jewels, are kept in the Jewel House at the Tower of London. They include crowns, swords, and scepters used on various state occasions. There are ten royal crowns on display, including the Imperial State Crown (see page 19). The Great Sword of State and the Jewelled Sword are accompanied by three Swords of Justice. There is also a collection of silver-gilt plates, most of which was made for Charles II at the Restoration.

Royal Parks

There are five royal parks near the center of London — Green Park, Hyde Park, Kensington Gardens, Regent's Park, and St. James's Park. Three other royal parks — Bushy, Greenwich, and Richmond — are further out. Many of these open spaces were originally royal hunting

grounds. St. James's Park is the oldest, being used in the early 16th century by Henry VIII for jousting and bowling. Hyde Park, the largest of the royal parks, became a fashionable place to visit after its opening in the early 17th century. By 2004, it will be home to the Diana, Princess of Wales Memorial Fountain.

EAST AND WEST END LONDON

1608 Hog's Lane is renamed Petticoat Lane (from sellers of old clothes).

1682 A license to establish Spitalfields market, the important vegetable market, is granted.

1705 Her Majesty's Theatre opens in

Haymarket (as Queen's Theatre).

1730 Bond Street is built from Piccadilly to Oxford Street.

1807 East London Waterworks Co. is founded.

1819 Burlington Arcade is built off Piccadilly.

1858 Brunel's Great Eastern (then the world's largest ship) is launched at an Isle of Dogs shipyard.

1864 The Garrick Club moves to the new Garrick Street, Covent Garden.

1868 Millwall dock opens.

1869 East London Railway trains run through the new Thames Tunnel.

1875 The original Liberty's store opens in Regent Street.

1904 Foyle's bookshop opens in Charing Cross Road.

1906 The Ritz Hotel opens in Piccadilly.

1910 Electrically lit signs are put up in Piccadilly Circus.

1930 Marks and Spencer open their Marble Arch store.

1931 The Dorchester

Different Classes

Well-to-do, middle-class Londoners began moving west from the City in Georgian times, (see pages 16–17). The West End soon became the center of government and fashionable London life. To the north and east of the City, workers lived in cheap housing, often far from where they worked. Many found work in the shipyards, as trade increased at the port of London's docks during the 18th and 19th centuries.

London is a vast and diverse city. Although the East and West Ends exist, it is difficult to mark them on a map.

Famous Museums

There are many famous museums and art galleries in and around the West End. One of the greatest tourist attractions is Madame Tussaud's waxworks collection in Marylebone Road. This world-famous attraction opened in 1835, and there are usually long queues to get in every day. A wide collection of decorative arts is held at the Victoria and Albert Museum, in South Kensington.

East and West End

London has two quite separate western and eastern districts, though neither is an official borough. The West End is so called because it is to the west of the City. This is where the middle classes moved in the 18th century, and it is now London's main entertainment and shopping area, with major theaters, cinemas, clubs, shops, and restaurants. The East End, to the other side of the City and extending east to Docklands, has always been less well off. Since the docks closed, some successful attempts have been made to regenerate the area with stylish office and apartment buildings, and shopping malls replacing run-down warehouses.

Piccadilly Circus

This famous West End landmark (right, photographed in the 1950s) took shape in 1819 at the spot where Piccadilly met the new Regent Street. The statue of Eros, originally representing an angel of charity, was unveiled in 1893 as a memorial to the Earl of Shaftesbury, the Victorian philanthropist. Today the circus is surrounded by shops and shopping malls.

The name Piccadilly comes from the ruffs worn by 17th-century English dandies such as this.

Above: Petticoat Lane in 1870, by which time the street's official name had changed to Middlesex Street. There is still a bustling Sunday market there today, on the eastern border of the City.

Hotel opens in Park Lane.

1962 Rebuilt St. Mary-le-Bow church (bombed in World War II) is completed.

1981 The London Docklands Development Corporation is set up.

1982 New Billingsgate fish market opens at the old

West India dock, Isle of Dogs.

1999 Jubilee line extension to underground railroad opens, connecting Canary Wharf.

2003 Building starts on a children's interactive bioscience center in London's East End.

Below: This Indian decoration for a pump organ of 1795 is exhibited in the V&A Museum.

Shopping

By the early 20th century London, and especially the West End, had become famous for its shops, and most of all for its department stores. Oxford Street developed into a shopping street, and the huge new Selfridge's store opened there in 1909. Five years later, 950 men and 2,550 women worked in its 160 departments. Regent Street, Bond Street, and Piccadilly offered more up-market shopping opportunities.

Right: An advertisement declaring the new Selfridge's store "open to the world."

Harrod's department store, in Knightsbridge, was first opened in the late 19th century. It is now one of the most prestigious stores in London.

London

Cockneys

True Cockneys are born within the sound of Bow Bells, the church bells of St. Mary-le-Bow in Cheapside, near St. Paul's. Cockneys are famous for their London accent, their cheeky banter, and especially their rhyming slang (boat race = face, mince pies = eyes). This is made more complicated and amusing by abbreviation: *'ave a butcher's* = have a look (butcher's hook); *up the apples* = up the stairs (apples and pears); *a new titfer* = a new hat (tit for tat).

Isle of Dogs

This area of East London is not really an island, but a peninsula on the north bank of the Thames created by a large bend in the river. It was the site of the important West India and Millwall docks, which closed in 1980. Billingsgate market was relocated there, and several printing works and the London Arena were built.

Right: View of the Isle of Dogs, looking across Mudchute Park to the old Millwall dock.

Young Cockney flower girl in an idealized setting in a painting by William Logsdail entitled St. Martin-in-the-Fields (1888).

Above: A typical East End back alley, photographed around 1902 in Bethnal Green.

Poverty

Up to Victorian times and beyond, many parts of the East End were full of overcrowded streets and narrow, dingy alleys. Everyone in the family had to work, including young children. Some youngsters worked as "mudlarks," scavenging the mud of the Thames (see pages 30–31) for objects of value, or anything that might fetch a few pence in the local market. Boys as young as four or five worked as "chummies" (chimneysweeps).

Theaterland

There are more than 30 mainstream theaters in the West End, stretching from Piccadilly to Aldwych. Most are long-established or even historic buildings, and they offer a range of entertainment, from serious drama to the latest hit musicals. The Theatre Royal, Drury Lane, in Covent Garden, was founded in 1663 and has existed in its present building since 1812.

An advertising poster of the early 1900s for the Prince's Theatre, which was renamed the Shaftesbury in 1962.

Right: Water jug celebrating the popular soap opera "EastEnders," situated in the fictitious Albert Square area of East London, which has been running successfully on British television since 1985.

Jack the Ripper

Within a period of three months in 1888, five women were murdered in the Whitechapel district east of the City. The unidentified murderer became known as "Jack the Ripper," because of the way he mutilated his victims. The police brought bloodhounds to the streets of Whitechapel, but the murderer was never found. There have since been many theories about his identity.

Right: This letter was sent to the police in October 1888 by an anonymous person claiming to be the Ripper. He enclosed half a human kidney preserved in wine.

Suffragettes

From 1903 a women's movement, led by Emmeline Pankhurst (1858–1928) and her daughters Christabel and Sylvia, demanded votes for women in the UK. Known as suffragettes, the women held public demonstrations in London, refused to pay taxes, and attacked property. Their efforts were rewarded in 1918, when women over the age of 30 were given the vote. Ten years later the voting age for women was lowered to 21, the same age as men.

Below: In 1914 Emmeline Pankhurst was arrested outside Buckingham Palace after trying to present a petition to the king.

World War I

When Britain declared war on Germany in 1914, after the German invasion of Belgium, cheering crowds surged through London. Young enthusiastic Londoners from all walks of life queued to "join up" (enlist in the army), unaware of the horrors they would face in the trenches. The following year, bombs began falling on London from Zeppelin airships (like the one shown right), and later from airplanes. Altogether there were 31 air raids on the capital, causing 670 deaths.

Recruiting poster. Conscription was introduced in 1916.

1901 – 1939

1901 Queen Victoria's eldest son comes to the throne as Edward VII.

1903 First service is held in the Roman Catholic Westminster Cathedral.

1906 Bakerloo underground railroad line opens.

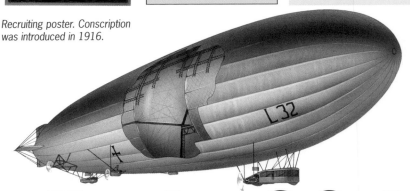

Early 20th

L ondon was a vibrant city in the first decade of the 20th century, but inevitably the mood changed during World War I (1914–18). Londoners' spirits rose again during the 1920s, as radio and cinema brought new forms of entertainment. There was a mass move toward the suburbs, as people searched for a higher standard of living. These new aspirations, however, were severely undermined by the Great Depression, and the effects of that economic crisis were still being felt when war once again changed and darkened everyone's daily life in 1939.

Edward VII in his royal robes.

Edwardian Era

Edward VII reigned until 1910, and the first decade of the 20th century is referred to in Britain as the Edwardian era. This popular monarch was born (and died) in Buckingham Palace, crowned in Westminster Abbey, and lay in state in Westminster Hall. There are nine statues of him in London. Edward became a leader of fashionable London society, and encouraged a more vibrant, active lifestyle than the Victorians enjoyed.

Empire Exhibition

In 1924 King George V (reigned 1910–36) opened the British Empire Exhibition at the newly completed Wembley Stadium. The opening ceremony was broadcast live on radio by the BBC. Fifty-six countries of the Empire took part in the patriotic exhibition, which included concrete pavilions for different countries, an amusement park, and a model coal mine, all connected by railroad. The exhibition ran into the following year (see poster, right), and altogether it was attended by 27 million people.

BBC

The British Broadcasting Corporation (or Company as it was then) put out its first radio programs from Marconi House in the Strand in 1922. The "wireless" quickly became more available and was very popular for news and entertainment by the 1930s. The first experiments in television had been made in 1926, and ten years later there were regular broadcasts from studios in Alexandra Palace, in north London. This created great excitement, but television did not become a popular

This early cover of The Radio Times, which gave information about BBC programs, shows a tranquil family setting.

force until after World War II. Nevertheless, throughout the 1920s and 30s, the BBC had an increasing influence on the everyday lives of the nation.

1907 Hampstead Garden Suburb is built.

1910 Edward VII's second son succeeds him as George V.

1913 Suffragettes set fire to Kew Tea Pavilion and attempt the same at the Royal Academy.

1915 Bombs fall on London from Zeppelin airships.

1917 British royal family changes its name from Saxe-Coburg-Gotha to Windsor.

1923 Wembley Stadium opens.

1924 Big Ben chimes and Greenwich time signals are broadcast on radio.

1925 American actor John Barrymore plays *Hamlet* at the Haymarket Theatre.

1929 Workhouses are abolished.

1931 The new Dorchester Hotel opens in Park Lane.

1932 The BBC moves to Broadcasting House, in Portland Place.

1933 The Open Air Theatre opens in Regent's Park.

1934 Battersea Power Station starts producing electricity.

1935 The Geological Museum opens in South Kensington.

1936 Senate House (main building of the University of London) opens.

1937 King George VI is crowned in Westminster Abbey. Earls Court exhibition hall is completed.

1939 The population of Greater London reaches 8.6 million. War is declared against Germany.

Houses on an LCC council estate.

Century

Suburbanization

During the 1920s and 30s the population of Greater London grew from 7.4 to 8.6 million, yet numbers in the inner city fell by 470,000 to 4 million. More people were moving out to the suburbs and commuting in to work. Roads and railroads continued to develop to make this possible. In London and its suburbs, new council estates were built — groups of houses built and rented out to tenants by the London County Council (LCC) and other local councils.

Cinema

The first London cinemas, such as the Electric Cinema in Portobello Road and the Electric Pavilion in Holloway Road, opened in 1910. Some theaters and music halls were also converted into silent-film cinemas before 1920. By then film production had already started at Ealing, in west London, and the famous Ealing Studios started producing "talkies" in 1931. Over the next seven years, around 60 feature films were made there.

Charlie Chaplin (right) (1889–1977) was born in London and became a stage performer there before going to Hollywood in 1914. He became a world star with films such as Modern Times (1936), in which he satirized the new machine age.

Great Depression

A terrible economic depression reached Britain from America in 1930. Like many other cities, London suffered greater unemployment and poverty than previously. Being the center of government, it was also the focus of protest. Many marches were organized, including the famous hunger march in 1936 from Jarrow, in northeast England, which was hit hard by the decline in shipbuilding. Such demonstrations increased political and social tension in the capital.

Below: This 1920s ginger jar is in the fashionable style of the time, Art Deco.

Below: This painting of 1903 shows the 231 main performers of the Edwardian music hall gathered in Waterloo Road, their traditional meeting place.

Edward VIII

London, along with the rest of the UK, was rocked in 1936 by events surrounding the new king. Edward VIII was determined to marry Mrs Wallis Simpson, but the fact that she was a divorcée meant that most politicians, including Prime Minister Stanley Baldwin, found her unacceptable as queen. Edward therefore decided to abdicate and hand the crown to his brother, who became George VI. Edward was given the title Duke of Windsor and married Mrs Simpson in France in 1937.

Right: There were frequent protest marches in London during the 1930s.

Left: Edward VIII and Wallis Simpson, who became Duke and Duchess of Windsor.

TRANSPORTATION

The driver of a hansom cab was seated behind the two passengers. The vehicle was named after the architect Joseph Hansom (1803–82), who patented it in 1834.

This Roman surveyor is using a special instrument to check that a road is level and straight.

Roman Roads

The great medieval markets at Cheapside and Eastcheap may have grown up on roads that were built many centuries before by the Romans. The present Watling Street, near St. Paul's, was probably part of *A double-decker bus.* the main Roman road from Dover to St. Albans. Many other roads within and leading from London had Roman origins, though later builders did not stick to the ancient practice of building them straight!

1803 Horse-drawn railroad opens from Wandsworth to Croydon. Commercial Road connects the City to the docks.

1815 First steamboat service on the Thames.

1837 Euston Station opens as London's first main-line railroad terminus.

1838 Horse-drawn omnibus drivers and conductors are licensed.

1842 Queen Victoria arrives at Paddington Station after her first railroad journey, from Slough.

1848 Waterloo Station opens.

Horse Power

The first horse-drawn omnibuses were introduced to London in 1829, and soon they could carry up to 18 passengers. By the end of the century there was competition from motorized vehicles, but horse buses did

not disappear until 1916. Throughout this time the two-wheeled hansom cab remained popular, and in 1900 there were 7,000 hansoms in London.

1897 The first motor bus is licensed.

1901 Electric trams are introduced (and run until 1952).

1904 The first double-decker bus and petrol-engine taxi are launched.

1926 The first traffic roundabout, at Parliament Square, is completed.

1933 London Passenger Transport Board is set up.

1958 Gatwick Airport opens.

The City Grows

During the Victorian era the introduction of horse-drawn omnibuses at affordable prices meant that Londoners were suddenly much more mobile. Then the advent of steam trains meant that people could

1969 The Queen opens the underground Victoria Line.

1977 The underground Piccadilly Line is extended to Heathrow Airport.

1979 The Prince of Wales opens the underground Jubilee Line.

move a reasonable distance from their place of work. Many moved to the green spaces at the edge of London and commuted in to work every day. Before long, the spaces between suburbs filled up, and the city sprawled and spread.

Transportation

During the 19th and 20th centuries London's growing public transportation system helped the city expand. Today, the system consists largely of overland trains, underground trains and buses, as well as licensed taxis. New, extended underground lines and additional bus lines have been introduced in recent years to cover new areas, and efforts are being made to cut down traffic jams in central London. A new congestion charge has been introduced for private cars driving into the center, encouraging commuters to switch to public transportation, in particular the "Tube," whose network of underground lines runs for miles under the streets of London.

1980 London Transport Museum opens in Covent Garden.

1986 Heathrow's Terminal Four opens.

1987 London City Airport opens between the former

Royal Albert and King George V docks. Docklands Light Railway opens. A fire in King's Cross underground station kills 31 people.

1991 Stansted Airport in Essex opens.

1995 Eurostar service to Paris begins at Waterloo.

2003 Congestion charge introduced for private motorists driving into London. Concorde makes its final flight, landing at Heathrow Airport.

Heathrow airport lies 14 miles (23 km) from the city center. In the 1980s, British Rail promoted their new railroad services to London's airports — Heathrow and Gatwick (right).

Railway to runway

Railroads

The first passenger train ran in London in 1836, between Bermondsey and Deptford, and the first main-line station opened the following year. The new form of transportation was enormously popular, and Londoners used it to visit

The Railway Station by William Powell Frith (1862) shows the dramatic hustle and bustle of Paddington Station, which was designed by the great engineer Isambard Kingdom Brunel.

friends and relatives in the country, then for day trips to the seaside, and finally to commute to work. The railroad simply changed the way people thought about travel. Today there are eight main railroad stations, all linking up with the underground system.

The Underground

The world's first underground trains ran in London in 1863. Before long there were 25 stops on the Metropolitan Inner-Circle Railway. The original trains used steam locomotives, but these filled the tunnels with smoke and steam. By 1890

River Services

Sailing boats and barges have carried people along the Thames for centuries, and steam-driven river buses were introduced in 1938. Today there are pleasure cruises between 15 piers from Hampton Court (see page 29) in the west to the Thames Barrier (see page 40) in the east. Faster commuter services operate to the center from Chelsea Harbour in the west and Docklands in the east. In 2003 a new river service opened between the Tate Britain art gallery at Millbank and the Tate Modern at Bankside.

This famous view of a Thames procession on Lord Mayor's Day was painted by Canaletto around 1747.

This painting by George William Joy entitled The Bayswater Omnibus (1895) shows passengers traveling in a horse-drawn omnibus near Hyde Park.

London's distinctive black cab.

they had been replaced by electric trains. Today there are 275 stations on 12 different underground or "tube" lines (color-coded on the distinctive map), covering more than 248 miles (400 km) of railway.

Above: A map of the eastbound Central Line on London's underground.

Black Cabs

London's licensed taxis are also known as black cabs, though some of them are different colors and others carry advertising. They all have a yellow "TAXI" sign on top, which is lit up when they are free. Would-be taxi drivers have to learn hundreds of routes that make up what they call "the knowledge" and then pass tests.

Heathrow Airport

Heathrow is the world's busiest international airport, flown to by more than 90 airlines. Its four terminals handle over 64 million passengers every year, and

Eurostar

Eurostar trains run from Waterloo International station to the center of Paris, France, and Brussels, in Belgium. There are 14 London-Paris services every day, and the Eurostar speeds through the Channel Tunnel to reach Paris in four hours.

there are plans for a fifth terminal. Heathrow opened as London Airport in 1946. Today it is connected to central London by an express rail service, as well as the Underground.

A high-speed Eurostar train.

ARCHITECTURAL STYLES

c. 70 The Roman forum and basilica are built.

c. 240 The Temple of Mithras is built.

604 First wooden St. Paul's church.

1067 Beginnings of the wooden Tower fortress.

1220 St. Mary Overie

church (later Southwark Cathedral) is rebuilt in Gothic style.

1446 Wooden chimneys are banned as a fire hazard.

1570 Tudor hall of the Middle Temple opens.

1615 Inigo Jones is

appointed surveyor-general of royal buildings.

1667 Rebuilding Act rules that large houses are to be no more than four storeys high.

1730s Berkeley Square is laid out.

1827 Marble Arch,

designed by John Nash, is put up in front of Buckingham Palace (and moved in 1851).

1845 Fountains complete Trafalgar Square.

1847 The Architectural Association is founded in the Strand.

1881 London's first garden suburb, Bedford Park, is completed.

1910 Admiralty Arch is built at the end of the Mall.

1951 Royal Festival Hall opens on the South Bank.

1976 The National Theatre opens on the South Bank.

Norman

After the early influences of Roman and Anglo-Saxon architecture, the style of London's major buildings changed considerably with the arrival of the Normans. The new style included rounded Romanesque arches and geometrical

decoration. The arches and sturdy round columns can still be seen at the church of St. Bartholomew-the-Great, which was founded by an Augustinian monk in 1123. The Temple Church, built 39 years later for the Knights Templar, shows a change towards the style known as Early English.

Gothic

From the 12th century the more decorated style of Gothic influenced important buildings, especially

A gargoyle (far left) from the Temple Church. Pointed arches in the Temple Church near Fleet Street show a development of the Norman style.

churches. Walls were thinner and taller, with high windows, arches, and towers. This style is evident in developments at Westminster Abbey, where the roof of the high nave was supported by flying buttresses.

Tudor

In the 16th century, when Henry VIII dissolved the monasteries and church buildings were transferred to the Crown (see page 12), styles changed. Wealthy people began building large, spacious manor houses. Brick started to replace

Below: Canaletto's painting of Henry VII's chapel at Westminster Abbey in the 18th century. Built between 1503 and 1512, it is a masterpiece of late-Gothic Perpendicular style.

Architectural Styles

The architecture of London has followed its turbulent history, with attempts made at various times to plan the city's growth. During the 17th century the effects of civil war, plague, and fire meant that the city had to be rebuilt, with bricks replacing timber. The sprawling suburbs grew largely during the 19th century. After 1945, areas that were heavily bombed during World War II again had to be rebuilt. Renovation and rebuilding schemes have assured that many of London's historic buildings have been preserved.

Regency

In 1811 the Prince Regent (future George IV) asked three architects for designs for a new development on the farmland of Marylebone Park. The winning design was put forward by John Nash (1752–1835), who

worked in many styles, from Gothic to Palladian. Nash proposed terraces and crescents around a new park. This became Regent's Park and included the creation of Regent Street, as well as Trafalgar Square and St. James's Park.

Below: John Nash's splendid Cumberland Terrace, overlooking Regent's Park, was completed in 1828.

1982 The Barbican Arts Centre opens.

2000 The Tate Modern art gallery (the converted Bankside power station) opens.

2002 Steel and glass City Hall (with offices for the elected mayor) opens near Tower Bridge.

The Great Gatehouse at Hampton Court, which was taken over by Henry VIII and became a royal palace in 1529.

For the last 25 years of his life, Sir Christopher Wren (1632–1723) (right) was surveyor-general of Westminster Abbey. He was buried in St. Paul's Cathedral.

stone, and plasterwork and carved wood became popular. One of the great Tudor buildings was Hampton Court, near London, which was originally intended as Cardinal Wolsey's (1475–1530), country residence. Another is St. James's Palace, at the end of Pall Mall, where Elizabeth I held court.

Palladian Style

The great architect Inigo Jones (1573–1652) was himself a Londoner, born in the City and christened in the church of St. Bartholomew-the-Less. On journeys to Italy, Jones studied the work of Andrea Palladio (1508–80), and he introduced the Palladian style to England. Inspired by classical Roman design, this style was based on a balanced harmony of proportions.

Left: The interior of the Banqueting House, in Whitehall. Designed by Inigo Jones and completed in 1622, this was the first Palladian building in London. The ceiling paintings are by Rubens.

St. Paul's Cathedral

Destroyed by the Great Fire of 1666, St. Paul's was rebuilt between 1675 and 1710. It was the greatest achievement of architect Christopher Wren, who rebuilt more than 50 churches in London. The cathedral's 361-feet (110 m) high dome has remained one of the city's most famous landmarks.

Though some of Wren's original design plans had been rejected, the grand, imposing structure of the new St. Paul's (right) was greatly admired. It was an amazing spectacle for 18th century Londoners.

Victorian

Many different styles were used during the great building works that took place in Victorian times. During the early part of the 19th century there was a revival of interest in classical Greek architecture. The British Museum was rebuilt in this Classical style. In contrast, the

The Houses of Parliament, at Westminster.

Houses of Parliament, which replaced the old Palace of Westminster that burned down in 1834, are in a style known as Gothic Revival. The new parliament building was begun in 1840, as the Museum neared completion.

Modern Design

In recent years different styles have been used for modern buildings, many of which are high-rise. Sir Richard Rogers' high-tech Lloyds Building (1986), with

all its service functions on the outside, was revolutionary. At 777 feet (237 m) tall, the pointed steel skyscraper at One Canada Square (1991), Canary Wharf, is London's tallest building.

Right: Canary Wharf is part of a redevelopment of London's Docklands area.

THE THAMES

1450 The newly elected Lord Mayor is rowed by barge with silver oars to Westminster.

1581 Elizabeth I knights Francis Drake at the Royal Naval Dockyard in Deptford.

1594 Elizabeth I gives Syon House, beside the river at Isleworth, to the Earl of Northumberland.

1664 Foundation stone laid for the Royal Naval College at Greenwich.

1715 First rowing of annual Doggett's Coat and Badge Race from London Bridge to Chelsea.

1802 West India Dock opens as the first large enclosed dock.

1843 The first Thames tunnel is completed, from Wapping to Rotherhithe.

1860 The Thames Rowing Club is founded.

1864 Hungerford Railway Bridge, including a footbridge, is completed.

1868 Millwall Dock opens on the Isle of Dogs.

1870 Victoria Embankment is completed.

1886 Tilbury Docks are opened.

1908 Port of London Authority is established.

1919 Naval river pageant celebrates the end of World War I.

1921 King George V Dock opens.

1937 National Maritime Museum opens in Greenwich.

The Route to London

The Thames flows through some famous towns and past many well-known landmarks before it reaches London. The river flows to the west of Oxford, where it is locally called the "Isis," before reaching Reading. Next it winds its way to Henley-on-Thames, site of an annual royal regatta that was first held on the river in 1839. The Thames then heads east, through Maidenhead and Windsor, flowing past Hampton Court before reaching west London.

Above: Windsor Castle was begun by William the Conqueror as a stockaded earthwork. The Queen still uses it as a royal residence today.

The Thames

The River Thames flows for 215 miles (346 km) from its source in the Cotswold Hills to its estuary, where it empties into the North Sea. Called "Tamesis" by Julius Caesar, the river was as important to the Roman settlers of Londinium as it has remained to this day. Its role as a transport route and source of water helped the small settlement grow into one of the world's great cities. Though its docks have now closed, the river is still seen as one of London's major features, flowing right through its center. Once badly polluted, the river has recently been cleaned up, and riverside homes and places to moor boats are greatly sought after.

The river is tidal downstream from Teddington, as water pushes in from the estuary, causing two high tides a day.

Above: Figurehead on the Cutty Sark, a 19th-century clipper ship that lies beside the river at Greenwich.

Beside the River

Many famous buildings and landmarks lie right beside the Thames in central London. These include: on the north bank, the Houses of Parliament, Cleopatra's Needle, Old Billingsgate fish market, and the Tower of London; on the south bank, the London Eye, Festival Hall, the National Theatre, the Tate Modern, and the Globe Theatre. Near Tower Bridge, the World War II battle cruiser HMS Belfast has been a floating naval museum since 1971.

Battersea Power Station was opened in 1933. Plans for its redevelopment are underway.

An atmospheric 19th-century postcard showing the Tower of London.

There are many famous riverside pubs. The historic Anchor (above) is near Southwark Bridge.

Events

The annual Lord Mayor's Show has often included a river procession, since this was first recorded in 1422. Many other regattas, pageants, and races have been held on the Thames. The most famous annual event is the University Boat Race, between the coxed eights of Oxford and Cambridge. This was first held at Henley in 1929, but 16 years later moved to London. The race is rowed from Putney to Mortlake, a distance of about 4 miles (7 km), and thousands of spectators line the riverbanks to cheer the rowers on.

Construction of St. Katharine's Dock began in 1827. It became one of the busiest docks along the Thames in the 19th century.

The Port of London Authority is still responsible for use of the river's facilities.

Port of London

By the 17th century, up to 90 percent of Britain's trade passed through the port of London. Then there was a great expansion of trade, as the British Empire grew, making London one of the world's busiest ports. By the end of the 18th century the quays were totally congested, and between 1802 and 1921 enclosed wet docks were built. After a period of great success, their use declined during the 20th century, until their eventual closure and redevelopment as the new Docklands area.

Below: The Oxford crew winning the 2002 Boat Race.

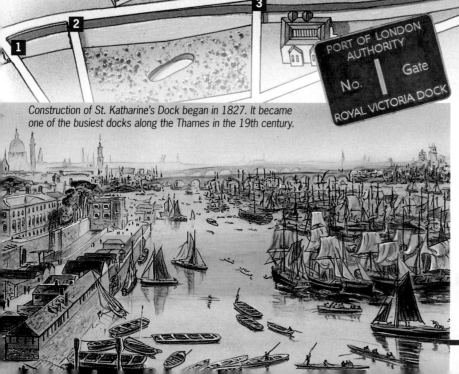

1971 London Bridge (completed in 1831) is reassembled and reopens at Lake Havasu City, Arizona, USA.

1973 St. Katharine's Dock is redeveloped as a marina.

1981 Royal Albert, Royal Victoria, and King George V docks close, leaving Tilbury to act as the Port of London.

2003 Oxford University win the Boat Race by just 30 cm. A new riverboat service opens between Millbank and Bankside.

Below: The frozen Thames in 1677.

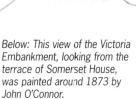

Shipbuilding

The building of large ships on the Thames began in 1513 when the Royal Naval Dockyard (or King's Yard) opened at Deptford to build a navy for Henry VIII. In the 1850s, the great engineer Isambard Kingdom Brunel built what was then the world's largest ship, the Great Eastern, at a new shipyard on the Isle of Dogs. A little further downstream was the home of the Thames Ironworks and Shipbuilding Company, which between 1846 and 1912 built about 900 vessels, including huge battleships.

A late 19th-century photograph of shipbuilding on the Thames probably showing engineers and shipyard owners.

London's Bridges

There are 16 road bridges between Richmond Bridge in the west and Tower Bridge in the east, as well as several rail and pedestrian bridges. The first crossing was the wooden London Bridge, replaced by stone in 1209 (see pages 10–11), while Westminster Bridge opened in 1750. The opening of a new bridge is always a major event, and the most recent was the Millennium footbridge (see page 43), which proved just how difficult bridge-building can be, even in the modern, high-tech age!

Pollution

Until the middle of the 19th century, people used the river as a garbage dump. It also received waste from sewers. In the hot summer of 1858, the river smelled so badly that it created the so-called "Great Stink." Even the windows of the Houses of Parliament had to be draped with sheets soaked in disinfectant. This led to a new system of sewers being built, which took waste much further downstream. In the following century industrial waste became a problem, but since the 1960s efforts have been made to clean up the Thames, resulting in the successful return of fish and waterbirds.

The deck of Tower Bridge, completed in 1894, opens in the middle to allow large ships to pass through.

Below: This view of the Victoria Embankment, looking from the terrace of Somerset House, was painted around 1873 by John O'Connor.

Right: A cartoon of 1858 derides the polluted river.

The River Thames
1 Battersea Bridge
2 Albert Bridge
3 Chelsea Bridge
4 Vauxhall Bridge
5 Lambeth Bridge
6 Westminster Bridge
7 Hungerford Railway Bridge
8 Waterloo Bridge
9 Southwark Bridge
10 London Bridge
11 Tower Bridge

The Embankments

The Albert, Chelsea, and Victoria Embankments, in central London, were built between 1864 and 1874. They were the work of the chief engineer to the Metropolitan Board of Works, Sir Joseph Bazalgette (1819–91), who also created London's new drainage system. A huge amount of land was reclaimed to build the embankments, involving clearing mud and building strong, high walls. Sewers and Underground railroad lines were laid beneath the new roads, and public gardens were added to make them more attractive.

1939 – 1945

1939 On September 3 war is declared. Winston Churchill is made First Lord of the Admiralty. St. Martin's School of Art (founded 1854) moves to Charing Cross Road.

1940 On May 10 Churchill becomes Prime Minister of a coalition government. On August 24 the first German bombs fall on central London. On October 15 a bomb hits Broadcasting House (but the radio announcer continues reading the news); small damage to St. Paul's Cathedral as fires rage around it. Iron railings are removed from parks and squares to use for munitions.

1941 May 10 is the last and worst night of the Blitz, with 3,000 Londoners killed. The Old Bailey and Corn Exchange are badly damaged. Women are called up to do vital jobs for the war effort.

1942 Fewer than 30 air raids on London. Some disused Underground stations become air-raid shelters.

1943 Exhibition called "Rebuilding Britain" is held at the National Gallery.

1944 The first V-1 flying bombs (nicknamed "doodlebugs") strike London, followed later by V-2 rockets. Glenn Miller and his famous band spend a night sheltering in Sloane Square tube station.

1945 Celebration of VE (Victory in Europe) day on May 8 and VJ (Victory over

Headline news on September 3, 1939.

Outbreak of War

On September 1, 1939 Hitler's troops invaded Poland. Two days later, at 11:15 in the morning, Prime Minister Neville Chamberlain broadcast to the British nation from the Cabinet Room at No. 10 Downing Street. He said that, since the German government had not replied to a note requiring them to withdraw the invading forces, "this country is at war with Germany." Less than half an hour later, the first air-raid siren went off in London — but it was a false alarm.

Above: Young London children in their air-raid shelter.

London at War

As Britain's largest city and center of government, London was an important target for German bombers during World War II. The most intensive period of bombing, lasting for more than eight months in 1940–41, reduced large areas of central London to rubble. Later in the war, the city was further hit by flying and rocket bombs. Despite the hardship and horror, many Londoners never lost their famous fighting spirit. When the war finally ended in 1945, Piccadilly Circus, Trafalgar Square, and many other famous landmarks were full of happy revelers.

Air-Raid Shelters

Many people with gardens were supplied with Anderson shelters, which were made mainly of corrugated iron. Others made do with an indoor Morrison shelter, which was like an iron cage with a strong top that acted as a table. There were also communal shelters in some basements, streets, and public parks, but these were dingy and unpopular. Many people preferred to spend the night on the platform of a Tube station, which was originally forbidden but became common by popular demand.

Churchill

In 1940, with the war going badly, the British government fell and Winston Churchill (1874–1965) became prime minister. Churchill gave memorable speeches in the House of Commons, and used all his energy and determination to encourage soldiers and civilians. With bombs falling on London, Churchill ignored air-raid warnings to visit the wounded. He toured military bases, with a large cigar in his mouth and his hand raised in his famous "V for victory" sign (above).

Above: Bomb damage in front of the Royal Exchange; the sign refers to a campaign encouraging people to grow their own vegetables.

Left: The poster is a paraphrase of a famous Churchill speech of 1940, just before the Battle of Britain.

Bomb Damage

Many parts of London were very badly damaged, and inevitably famous buildings were hit. On May 10, 1941 the House of Commons chamber was reduced to rubble, while Mansion House and the Tower of London were badly damaged. Even part of Buckingham Palace was bombed in 1940. In 1944 there was a new threat — V-1s and V-2 rocket-powered flying bombs. The bomb damage also caused unwanted but serendipitous excavation, uncovering sections of the Roman city wall and other archeological treasures.

Fire-fighters' equipment used during the Blitz.

The Blitz

On September 7, 1940, 348 German bombers escorted by 617 fighter planes bombed East London, causing huge destruction. This was the beginning of the London Blitz (from *Blitzkrieg*, meaning "lightning war"). The city was attacked every day or night for the next two months. By May 11, 1941, when bombing ended, 20,000 people had been killed and 1.4 million people had been made homeless by 71 major air raids.

Fire surrounds St. Paul's Cathedral, which amazingly suffered little damage.

Japan) day on August 15; there are street parties and festivities throughout London.

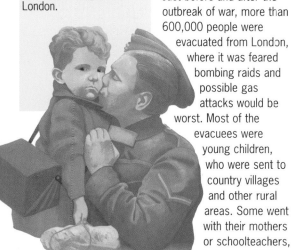

Children were evacuated with just a few belongings, a gas mask and a name tag.

Evacuation

Just before and after the outbreak of war, more than 600,000 people were evacuated from London, where it was feared bombing raids and possible gas attacks would be worst. Most of the evacuees were young children, who were sent to country villages and other rural areas. Some went with their mothers or schoolteachers, but many children also went alone.

Air Defence

In the first half of 1940 there was a real fear among Londoners that Hitler was planning to invade southern Britain. The RAF (Royal Air Force), though outnumbered by the German air force, managed to resist and defeat raids by German fighter planes. They fought a series of air battles between August and October 1940, known as the Battle of Britain. British pilots, in their Spitfire and Hurricane fighter aircraft, won the battle, though bombing was to continue.

Above: Spitfires flying over London.

Memorials

There are many war memorials in London, such as the RAF memorial at Victoria Embankment and the London Troops memorial at the Royal

The Cenotaph was designed by Sir Edwin Lutyens.

Exchange. The Cenotaph, in Whitehall, was built in 1920 to commemorate the dead of World War I. On Remembrance Day (the Sunday nearest November 11 — the day World War I ended) the dead of both World Wars and later conflicts are commemorated in a service attended by the Queen and the Prime Minister.

Right: The George Cross was instituted in 1940 by King George VI as a decoration for bravery awarded to civilians.

Left: Women training as voluntary firefighters in 1942.

Women at Work

As in World War I, the fact that most men had been conscripted into the armed forces meant that women had to take over their jobs in factories, shops, and offices. Many worked in munitions factories, making shells and bullets, while others drove lorries and buses. Some women pilots worked for the Air Transport Auxiliary, flying airplanes from factories to RAF bases throughout Britain.

Celebrating the End

After a long and tiring war, in which almost 30,000 Londoners had been killed and a third of the city completely destroyed, VE Day (Victory in Europe) was celebrated throughout the world on May 8, 1945. Dancing and singing, people packed the Mall and Whitehall, shouting "We want the King." Later, on VJ Day (Victory over Japan), August 15, Londoners celebrated once again, as they looked forward to a new beginning.

Right: Happy Londoners celebrate the end of the war on VE Day, 1945.

Olympics

The first Olympic Games after the war were awarded to London, where the facilities were not brilliant. A temporary running track was laid at Wembley Stadium. Due to housing shortages, the 3,700 male competitors were put up at RAF and army camps, and the 385 female competitors in colleges. Nevertheless, a record 59 countries attended.

Youth Culture

In the 1950s the growing number of young people in London began to change social attitudes. Young audiences were influenced by American films about rebels, such as *The Wild One* (1954) with Marlon Brando. Some young men became Teddy boys, dressing in a supposedly Edwardian, pseudo-respectable fashion. This usually included narrow "drainpipe" trousers and a smart jacket.

Right: A 1950s London "Ted."

Festival of Britain

This celebration was held in 1951, exactly a hundred years after the Great Exhibition (see page 19), to demonstrate Britain's post-war development in design and technology, and to give an exciting view of the future. The main site was on

Protests

During the 1950s and 1960s the Campaign for Nuclear Disarmament (CND) organized many sit-down protests outside the Ministry of Defence building in Whitehall and elsewhere in

Rebuilding

There was a terrible housing shortage after the war, since so many people had been made homeless. Planning schemes concentrated on redeveloping old slums as well as bombed areas. Some new neighborhood schemes went ahead, such as the Lansbury Estate in Poplar (see poster, right). This was the exhibit of living architecture at the Festival of Britain and was described in the press as "a modern oasis set in a vast area of overcrowded streets."

derelict land on the south bank of the Thames, where modern buildings were put up, including the Royal Festival Hall. Pleasure gardens were also laid out in Battersea Park. The five-month festival was a great success, attracting over eight million visitors.

London. There was also an annual 50-mile (80 km) march from Aldermaston in Berkshire to Trafalgar Square, where marchers were addressed by prominent campaigners such as Bertrand Russell.

LANSBURY·POPLAR

1945 – 1965

1945 End of World War II.

1945 End of World War II.

1946 Nazi propagandist William Joyce (Lord Haw-Haw) is hanged at Wandsworth Prison.

1947 Yellow lines are introduced to show parking restrictions.

1948 Dutch sprinter

United Nations

The new organization of the United Nations was founded at the end of the war in 1945. The first meeting of the UN General Assembly was held at St. James's Palace, London, where it was

Fanny Blankers-Koen wins four gold medals at the London Olympics.

1949 Laurence Olivier produces Tennessee Williams' *A Streetcar Named Desire* at the Aldwych Theatre.

1950 The rebuilt House of Commons is opened by

agreed that its permanent headquarters should be built in New York.

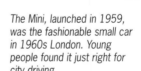

The United Nations flag.

Post-War London

After the war, London's widespread bomb damage led to efforts toward a more planned approach to building and development. New neighborhoods were designed, replacing bomb sites and old Victorian slums, especially in the East End. Despite the success of pilot housing-estate schemes associated with the successful Festival of Britain, high-rise blocks were also built. At the same time, eight new satellite towns were planned and built near London, relieving housing pressure in the capital to some extent. By the end of this period, however, many manufacturing industries were closing down or moving out of London, causing unemployment to rise.

The Mini, launched in 1959, was the fashionable small car in 1960s London. Young people found it just right for city driving.

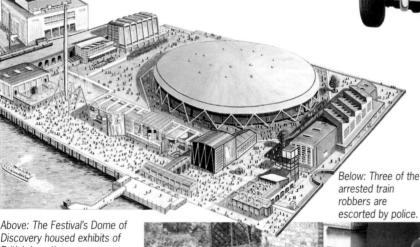

Above: The Festival's Dome of Discovery housed exhibits of British invention.

Below: Three of the arrested train robbers are escorted by police.

Great Train Robbery

On August 8, 1963 15 masked men stopped the night mail train from Glasgow to London and stole £2.5 million. This quickly became known as the "Great Train Robbery." Some of the gang, many of whom were from London, were arrested and sent to jail. The crime captured the public imagination, and the criminals became folk heroes.

Left: A CND protestor is removed by a policeman in 1962.

King George VI.

1951 Soviet double-agents Guy Burgess and Donald Maclean disappear.

1952 George VI (1895–1952) is succeeded by his 25-year-old daughter, Elizabeth.

1953 The Queen's coronation. The Samaritans organization is founded at St. Stephen Walbrook church.

1954 Bomb-site excavation reveals the Roman Temple of

Mithras. Food rationing ends.

1955 Samuel Beckett's *Waiting for Godot* is staged at the Arts Theatre Club.

1956 The Clean Air Act is passed. The Russian Bolshoi Ballet appears for the first time at the Royal Opera House.

Rock 'n' Roll

Rock 'n' roll came from America, and by the early 60s London had its own young bands, such as the Rolling Stones, Kinks, and Small Faces. Other British groups soon migrated to the capital, to record, perform,

1958 The Planetarium opens in Marylebone Road.

1959 Britain's first highway, the M1, opens north of London. Parking meters are introduced in London.

1960 Riots in St. Pancras over a new council rent scheme. Compulsory

and live. The Beatles (left), from Liverpool, played at the London Palladium in 1963 and took the capital by storm. Two years later they went to Buckingham Palace to receive MBEs (an honorary title — Member of the British Empire) from the Queen.

National Service is abolished.

1961 Satirical magazine *Private Eye* is published from Soho.

1962 The Shell Building opens on the South Bank.

1964 Martin Luther King gives a sermon at St. Paul's

The Coronation

The eyes of the whole country, and many across the world, were on London for Queen Elizabeth II's coronation in 1953. This was one of the first major events to be televised live.

Cathedral. Barbara Hulanicki opens her Biba boutique in Kensington, which later became one of the most fashionable stores in 1960s London.

1965 Funeral service for Sir Winston Churchill at St. Paul's Cathedral.

Around 30,000 people camped out on the London streets to get a good view, and stands holding 100,000 people were put up along the route of the procession from Buckingham Palace to Westminster Abbey.

Left: Stephen Ward, a London osteopath who was also involved in the Profumo scandal and committed suicide the same year.

Political Scandals

After revelations of Soviet spies in high places of the British establishment in the 1950s, another huge scandal blew up in 1963. The Conservative politician and secretary of state for war, John Profumo, was forced to resign when it was discovered that he had had an affair with Christine Keeler, who had also been involved with a Soviet naval attaché.

Following the Profumo scandal, Christine Keeler (above) was imprisoned for nine months.

Above: The Queen in her golden carriage on coronation day. After the horror of World War II, the coronation was a happy occasion for Londoners.

Right: This British Rail poster encouraged people to visit London in the year of the Queen's coronation.

55 BC – 43 AD Roman invasions of Britain.

1096 Jewish refugees from the Rouen pogrom arrive.

1500 Gypsies start to arrive in small numbers.

1517 On "Evil May Day," foreign merchants' shops

are attacked by a mob.

1555 First black slaves are brought from Africa.

1780 Lord George Gordon leads anti-Catholic riots.

1851 Around 100,000 make up the Irish community, mainly refugees

from the potato famine.

1898 London Irish Rugby Football Club is founded (after London Scottish in 1878 and London Welsh in 1885).

1902 Sikh *gurdwara*, a Hindu temple, opens in Shepherds Bush.

1908 First Chinese restaurant opens near Piccadilly Circus.

1924 The UK Buddhist Society is founded.

1927 First Indian restaurant is established in Regent Street by the great-grandson of an English general and an

Indian princess.

1932 Jewish Museum is founded in Tavistock Square.

1936 In the "Battle of Cable Street," Communists and Jews face off Fascists.

1958 Clashes between black and white residents in

Immigrants have played a major part in the history of London, which was once called the "city of nations." Its role as a port has always made it a major point of entry to Britain, and many have arrived looking for work and a new life, or seeking refuge from persecution. From early times, London has been home to groups of immigrants — from Jewish traders who arrived in the medieval period to Irish people fleeing starvation in the 19th century. After the 16th century, many immigrants were attracted to London because their homeland became part of the growing British Empire. This has resulted in the creation of a multicultural city, with traditional events, entertainment, and restaurants from all over the world.

Multicultural London

Early Immigrants

During the thousand years between the Roman invasions and the Norman conquest of 1066, the Celtic Britons who lived in the settlement of London were joined by many others. First there were Germanic tribes of Jutes, Angles, and Saxons, before Viking raiders arrived in the 9th century. During this period London became an increasingly important trading port, making it attractive to newcomers. These early immigrants were all absorbed into the population of the growing city.

Jewish Immigrants

Jewish people arrived from France soon after the Norman conquest, and there was a small Jewish quarter in London by the 12th century. The community was brutally expelled in 1290, and it was almost 400 years before Jews felt able to resettle openly. The next period of Jewish immigration followed their persecution in Russia and Poland after 1881, and more arrived during the 1930s. Many settled in the East End, where they played a major role in tailoring as well as finance.

The Great Synagogue was built to the east of the City in 1692 by German and Polish Jews.

Below: This 11th-century carved Viking stone was found at St. Paul's churchyard.

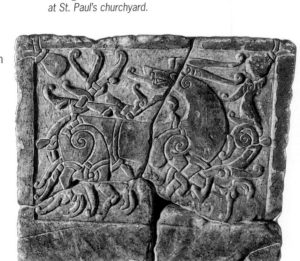

Chinatown

The first Chinese to settle in London were employees of the East India Company. By the 1880s Chinese

seamen had created a community in the Limehouse district, and many went into the laundry business. The district was badly bombed during World War II, and the Hong Kong Chinese and others who arrived in the 1960s turned to the West End area around Gerrard Street, where many opened restaurants and shops. This became the new Chinatown, which has since become a successful tourist attraction.

Below: Restaurants in Chinatown.

Left: Chinese sailors unload tea at the East India Docks in 1877.

Notting Hill.

1966 Caribbean Arts Movement is co-founded by Trinidadian publisher John La Rose.

1978 London Central Mosque is completed on the edge of Regent's Park.

1985 Ismaili (Muslim)

Huguenots

During the 14th and 15th centuries there was an influx of Hanseatic merchants, as well as weavers from Flanders. During the 1560s thousands of Huguenots (French Protestants) fled Catholic persecution, and many made their way to London. After losing their freedom of worship in

West Indies

A manpower shortage after World War II led to workers being invited from the Caribbean. In 1948 a former troopship called the Empire Windrush carried 492 young migrants from Jamaica to London. They were housed at a shelter in Clapham before being given a civic reception in Brixton. These first immigrants were

Right: A West Indian Seafood Festival in the Docklands.

The Irish

The Great Irish Famine of 1845–50, when potato harvests failed, led to hundreds of thousands of people being forced to leave their homeland. Some arrived on "coffin ships" in London, taking up poorly paid jobs in the docks or East End workshops. The Irish community grew in numbers and spirit, and has become especially associated with music. There is an exciting parade each St. Patrick's Day, which is attended and enjoyed by many non-Irish Londoners.

Centre opens in South Kensington.

1990 First Irish *fleadh* (music festival) is held in Finsbury Park.

2003 Special exhibition for Refugee Week at the Museum of Immigration and Diversity in Spitalfields.

France in 1685, many more Huguenots joined the earlier refugees. By 1700 there was a community of around 23,000 in Spitalfields, worshiping in nine Huguenot churches. Many of the immigrants were skilled silk weavers, while others were clockmakers, glass-blowers, and engravers.

A silk jacket made by Huguenot weavers in the East End.

followed by many others, and by 1966 a local Caribbean pageant and fair had grown into the annual Notting Hill Carnival.

Indian food is very popular in London.

Left: An Irish harp. Music remains an important tradition of the Irish community.

Below: In 1972 Smithfield Market porters joined an anti-immigration march through London. The

South Asia

Around the start of British direct rule of India in 1858, small communities of Indian seamen settled near the London docks. Some went on to become traders in the surrounding markets. By the 1920s, Indian professional people and students came to London, many for short stays. Major immigration from the subcontinent began after Indian independence and partition in 1947. The newcomers included

teachers, doctors, and ex-army officers, while many workers settled in Southall and other industrial districts.

Cultural Impact

Religion has been the focus of many immigrant communities. The present *Jamme Masjid* in Brick Lane has a remarkable history: it was built in 1743 as a Huguenot chapel, and was turned into a synagogue, and then a Methodist church before becoming a mosque. In Southall, the largest Sikh *gurdwara* outside India

A restaurant in Brick Lane, Spitalfields, which is the center of London's Bengali district.

opened in 2003, with room for 3,000 worshipers and an associated arts and cultural center. Other cultural institutions have a more secular approach. The Africa Centre, in Covent Garden, opened in 1964 to act as a forum for visiting Africans as well as those settled in London.

The Shri Swaminarayan Hindu temple and cultural complex, which opened in Neasden in 1995.

placard refers to Enoch Powell, a Conservative politician who spoke out against immigration.

Conflict

Unfortunately there has been a history of conflict associated with immigration. In the 1930s Fascist "Blackshirts" held anti-Jewish marches, which led to trouble in the East End, where the Fascists were given short shrift. Thirty years later, the extreme right-wing National Front party began a propaganda campaign in support of racial discrimination and opposing immigration. In 1999 many people were injured in nail-bomb attacks on Brixton and Brick Lane, thought to be aimed at local black and Asian communities.

Centuries ago most sports and leisure activities were practiced almost exclusively by wealthy Londoners. Hunting, bowls, and even tennis were popular pastimes with royalty. The famous street called Pall Mall took its name from an Italian game similar to croquet, for which it was set aside. Poorer people had little leisure time, yet they were still able to indulge in traditional games and enjoy themselves in pubs and music halls. In recent times, London has become a world-famous venue for sports events and other entertainments, including classical and popular music. Locals and visitors find a wealth of possibilities on offer, either as participants or spectators.

Cocks fought to the death in the cockpit, urged on by their gambling supporters.

SPORTS AND LEISURE

1393 The first pub signs are introduced outside medieval inns.

1437 The Brewers' Company is granted a charter.

1641 The Stag brewery opens in Westminster.

1747 A boxing academy

Traditional Games

In medieval times Londoners who could spare the time enjoyed a variety of leisure pursuits. These included ball games, archery, bowls, jousting, wrestling, and even skating on the Thames in freezing winters. There were also several bloodthirsty spectator "entertainments," such as cockfighting and bull-baiting. People gambled heavily on cockfights, which were sometimes held in pubs. In 1609 the Cockpit opened in Covent Garden especially for cockfighting, though it was converted into a theater seven years later.

Sports & Leisure

Union Jack flags are waved at the famous "Last Night of the Proms" (below) at the Royal Albert Hall (shown, left, in its original design).

Classical Music

The most celebrated London venues for classical music concerts are the Royal Festival Hall and the Royal Albert Hall. The famous Promenade Concerts (or "Proms"), so called because some of the audience stand rather than sit, were first held in the old Queen's Hall, but today they are an annual feature at the Albert Hall. The Proms were instituted by London-born conductor Sir Henry Wood in 1895.

opens beside Haymarket Theatre.

1814 Marylebone Cricket Club moves to Lord's cricket ground.

1835 Animal fighting is made illegal.

1872 First FA Cup final is played at the Oval.

1877 First Wimbledon tennis championships.

1880 First international cricket match in England is played at the Oval.

1884 First women's tennis matches at Wimbledon.

1908 Twickenham Rugby

Football Ground opens. Olympic Games are held at Shepherds Bush.

1910 The London Palladium opens as a music hall.

1923 FA Cup final played at Wembley Stadium for the first time.

1932 London Philharmonic Orchestra is formed by Sir Thomas Beecham.

1941 Promenade Concerts move to the

Royal Albert Hall.

1966 First Notting Hill Carnival is held.

1975 West Indies beat Australia in the first ever cricket World Cup final at Lord's.

1977 Wimbledon Lawn Tennis Museum opens.

1981 First running of the London Marathon.

1985 Live Aid charity concert held in London and Philadelphia.

2002 Wembley Stadium is demolished, to be replaced by a new National Stadium.

Pubs

England is famous for its pubs (short for "public houses"), and there are certainly plenty of them in London! They developed from the alehouses, inns, and taverns that have always existed in and around the city. Many of the most famous pub names have been around for many centuries, displayed on illustrated signs (right) so that places to eat, drink, and stay the night could be easily identified, even by those who couldn't read. The signs often display a brewer's name, too. John Charrington began brewing in the East End in 1766.

Below: This painting of 1882 shows the scene in a Victorian pub.

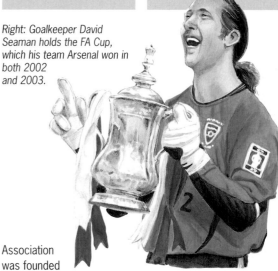

Right: Goalkeeper David Seaman holds the FA Cup, which his team Arsenal won in both 2002 and 2003.

Football

In medieval England, the game of football was twice banned — first for being too rough, and then for stopping young men from practicing archery. The Football Association was founded in 1863, and today is based in Soho Square. The first London club to win the English league was Arsenal in 1931. They were joined as champions by Tottenham Hotspur in 1951 and Chelsea in 1955. These three clubs remain the most successful in London today.

Festivals

From the 16th to the 19th centuries winter festivals, called Frost Fairs, were held on the Thames whenever it froze over. This happened behind the old London Bridge, where the water slowed. Today, an autumn festival is still held by the Pearly Kings and Queens, who represent the city's traditional traders and wear

A flamboyant Notting Hill Carnival costume.

clothes studded with pearl buttons. In late August, the Notting Hill Carnival fills the streets of that district with costumed parades and Caribbean fun.

Pop Music

In Victorian times many music halls opened in London. Street musicians also entertained with their barrel organs. During the

20th century London was at the forefront of developments in pop music. The Rolling Stones formed their band and began playing in the capital in 1963. In the 1970s, when

punk rock took over, the London group the Sex Pistols were a leading force. During the 1980s and 90s huge open-air concerts were common at Wembley Stadium. Today's

Above: View of the pavilion at Lord's in the late 19th century.

major indoor venues are London Arena (on the Isle of Dogs) and Wembley Arena. Since 1997, the Prince's Trust has hosted the "Party in the Park" in Hyde Park, a one-day pop concert.

Tennis

The Wimbledon Championships form the oldest and most famous international tennis tournament in the world. It was first played on the grass courts of the All England Croquet and Lawn Tennis Club at Wimbledon, in

Left: Clarence Clemons and the E Street Band accompanied Bruce Springsteen at Wembley in 1985. In 2003, "the Boss" played to sell-out crowds at Crystal Palace.

Cricket

The Marylebone Cricket Club (or MCC) was founded in 1787, and its home at Lord's cricket ground in St John's Wood became the headquarters of world cricket. The Middlesex

southwest London, in 1877. Then there were few competitors and just a few hundred spectators, but now those who manage to get tickets come from all over the world. It is the only one of the four major tournaments still to be played on grass.

county club plays at Lord's, while Surrey plays at the Oval ground in Kennington. Test matches between international teams are played at both grounds. Each test match lasts five days, yet games still often end in a draw!

Below: Wimbledon program from 1968 and ticket from 1911. Tickets for Centre and Number One courts are highly sought after.

Left: This painting of a Hackney tower block by Julian Perry is entitled The Enchanted Castle.

Now known as Baroness Thatcher, Margaret Thatcher (below) was prime minister throughout the 1980's, a boom time for London.

Margaret Thatcher

"Maggie" Thatcher (left) first entered the House of Commons as a member of parliament in 1959. She was elected leader of the Conservative Party in 1975, and four years later became the first woman prime minister of the UK. Her tough policies led to her being known as the "Iron Lady." After three terms in office, she was forced to resign and entered the House of Lords as a baroness in 1992.

1965 – 1999

1965 Greater London Council is formed. 620-feet (189 m) high Post Office (now Telecom) Tower is completed.

1966 London model Twiggy (born Lesley Hornby) is named "Face of the Year." The Shelter campaign for the homeless is founded.

Live Aid

In 1985 Irish singer Bob Geldof (right), star of the Boomtown Rats band, organized a massive charity concert held jointly at Wembley Stadium, London, and JFK Stadium in Philadelphia, USA. Stars such as David Bowie, Bob Dylan, Mick Jagger, and Paul McCartney helped raise millions of pounds for famine relief in Ethiopia.

Housing Development

In the mid-60s tower blocks became ever more popular with architects and developers, but a disaster in 1968 made people think again. A gas explosion on the 18th floor of the new 33-story Ronan Point in Newham, East London, damaged and partly destroyed the building. Four people were killed and 17 injured. Many residents found life in tower blocks lonely and anonymous.

Late 20th Century

During the 1960s, "swinging" London became one of the world's most fashionable cities. The trendy boutiques of the King's Road and Carnaby Street led the way in the age of the mini-skirt. This caused a rise in tourism, which continued to grow throughout the rest of the century. The experiments with high-rise housing estates were generally unpopular, failing to solve the growing problems of homelessness. During the 1980s there was a rise in the number of young, high-earning city-workers, yet at the same time there were more homeless people begging and sleeping on the streets. London's contrasts continued.

The Swinging Sixties

During the 1960s London became famous around the world as a swinging city at the forefront of young, modern fashion. Mary Quant, who was born in London in 1934 and studied at Goldsmiths' College of Art, had opened her first boutique in the King's Road, Chelsea, in 1955. She went on to pioneer the mini-skirt in the 60s.

Introduced in 1965, the mini-skirt dominated young women's fashion for the rest of the decade.

Silver Jubilee

Queen Elizabeth II celebrated her Silver Jubilee (25 years on the throne) in 1977. She attended a service of thanksgiving at St. Paul's Cathedral, and there were around 5,000 street parties in the capital. The Queen made many appearances and opened the new Jubilee Gardens on the South Bank.

Above: Silver Jubilee commemorative plate.

Yuppies bought the earliest mobile phones, which were expensive. Mobiles came into regular use in the 1990s.

Yuppies

During the 1980s London's business and financial services developed rapidly. This led to many young people earning large sums in the City, swelling the number of London's so-called "yuppies" (young urban professionals). These middle-class high-earners, trying to get rich quick before their stressful jobs burned them out, had a luxurious lifestyle.

Flood Barrier

After a tidal surge caused terrible flooding in the Thames estuary in 1953, it was decided that London needed protection from very high tides. This was achieved in 1984, when the Thames Barrier opened to the east of the Isle of Dogs. The 1,706 feet (520 m) wide steel barrier has a series of ten gates that can be raised when there is a flood alert. The gates rest on the riverbed when they are not needed, so that ships can pass into and out of London.

Right: Steel pier roofs, which look like shells, cover machines that open and close the gates of the Thames Barrier.

1967 East India docks close.

1968 Hayward Gallery opens on the South Bank.

1970 The old teahouse in Hyde Park opens as the Serpentine Gallery. Opening of the Westway urban highway.

1971 Centre Point office block is completed and stays empty for years.

1974 The Covent Garden fruit market moves to Nine Elms. Several IRA bombs go off in London.

1976 The Museum of London opens.

1977 The Public Record Office moves to Kew.

1981 The London Docklands Development Corporation is set up.

1983 The City of London elects its first Lady Mayor.

1985 Riots in Brixton and Tottenham.

1986 The M25 orbital highway around London is completed. The "Big Bang" brings electronic trading to the Stock Exchange.

1988 A Roman amphitheater is excavated at Guildhall Yard.

1993 London-born fashion designer Alexander

McQueen presents his first commercial collection at the Ritz Hotel.

1994 A giant new water ring main is completed beneath the city.

1995 The revamped Oxo Tower opens near Blackfriars Bridge.

1997 The new British Library opens at St. Pancras. Old offices and warehouses in Clerkenwell are turned into loft-conversion flats.

1998 The new Sadler's Wells Theatre opens.

1999 The Jubilee Line tube extension opens.

Carnaby Street, near Regent Street in the West End, became famous for its trendy boutiques and lively scene.

A Young Prime Minister

Tony Blair entered parliament in 1983 and became leader of the opposition Labour Party in 1994. Three years later he won a landslide general election victory at the age of 43, becoming the UK's youngest prime minister since Lord Liverpool in 1812. There was great celebration in London among Labour supporters, whose party had been out of power for 18 years, as Blair entered 10 Downing Street with his family (right).

Docklands

After the working docks in east London closed in the 1960s, little was done to redevelop the area for some time. Things got moving in the 1980s, however, and a resurrected area called Docklands slowly became a reality. The tall tower at Canary Wharf (see page 29) was completed in 1991, and the opening of the Docklands Light Railway made the area more accessible.

A driverless Light Railway train at Canary Wharf station.

1999 – PRESENT

1999 Preparations are made for celebrating the millennium, including the ill-fated Dome. Railroad crash at Ladbroke Grove kills 31 people. An official inquiry into the death of Stephen Lawrence, murdered by youths in Eltham, is opened.

2000 Millennium Bridge opens and promptly closes. London Eye starts turning. Tate Modern gallery opens. Docklands Light Railway extension to Lewisham. London Wetland Centre opens in Barnes. Mile End Park

opens beside Regent's Canal. The new Great Hall at the British Museum opens. Millennium Dome closes on December 31.

2001 Nelson Mandela opens a new refectory, library, and visitor center at

Southwark Cathedral. A new Education Centre opens at London Zoo.

2002 Millennium Bridge reopens (without wobble). Two new footbridges also open at Hungerford Railway Bridge. Greater London Authority moves into new City Hall.

2003 New Museum in Docklands opens, as part of the Museum of London. Announcement that London will bid to host the 2012 Olympics. Discussions continue on a possible fifth terminal for Heathrow Airport. Illusionist David Blane spends 44 days suspended over the Thames in a plexi-glass box.

Millennium Celebrations

As in other cities around the world, the new millennium was celebrated in London with great festivities on the night of December 31 1999/January 1 2000. This was the focus of UK celebrations. Huge crowds gathered in the center of the city to watch a spectacular fireworks display that began at midnight and included turning the Thames into a "river of fire."

Below: Fireworks lit up the night sky as Big Ben chimed midnight to announce the first day of the new year, new century, and new millennium.

Euro notes and coins took over from 12 national currencies in 2002. The UK continued to ponder the question, as traditionalists waged a "Save our pound" campaign.

The Euro Debate

Along with Denmark and Sweden, the UK decided not to adopt the new European single currency in 2002. Since then, the Chancellor of the Exchequer has announced in the House of Commons that economic conditions are not right for the UK to change its pound for the euro. At the same time, the prime minister promised that there would eventually be a national referendum on the issue.

Into the 21st

Eight hundred years after the first Lord Mayor became chief magistrate of the City of London, all Londoners had the chance to vote for their first directly elected mayor. This historic event led London into the new millennium, after all the exciting celebrations at the very end of the 20th century. Numerous buildings were created or renovated specially for the beginning of the third millennium, some more successfully than others. There are plans for many more new buildings and developments, ensuring that the London skyline will change just as much in the future as it always has in the past.

The British Museum

When the new British Library opened at St. Pancras in 1998, it was decided that the round Reading Room of the British Museum in Bloomsbury would be developed. The interior of the Reading Room has been restored to its original splendor, and around it a Great Court with a steel-lattice lightweight roof, designed by Sir Norman Foster, was built. This innovative design has created the largest covered courtyard in Europe.

The round Reading Room seen from inside the Great Court.

Right: The London Eye was designed by British husband-and-wife team David Marks and Julia Barfield, and parts were built in the Czech Republic, France, Germany, Italy, and the Netherlands, as well as the UK.

The London Eye

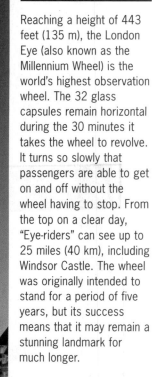

Reaching a height of 443 feet (135 m), the London Eye (also known as the Millennium Wheel) is the world's highest observation wheel. The 32 glass capsules remain horizontal during the 30 minutes it takes the wheel to revolve. It turns so slowly that passengers are able to get on and off without the wheel having to stop. From the top on a clear day, "Eye-riders" can see up to 25 miles (40 km), including Windsor Castle. The wheel was originally intended to stand for a period of five years, but its success means that it may remain a stunning landmark for much longer.

Tate Modern

The new Tate Modern gallery occupies the stark building of the former Bankside power station, which closed in 1981. Ready for its opening in 2000, the Tate's collection of international modern art was moved from its site on Millbank (now Tate Britain, see page 14). The Tate Modern has held highly successful special exhibitions, including the Surrealists, Picasso, and Matisse.

Right: This bronze work by English sculptor Henry Moore, Maquette for Madonna and Child, *can be seen in the Tate Modern.*

Century

New Mayor

In 2000, Londoners voted for their first ever directly elected mayor, to preside over a 25-member assembly. The election was won by the former Labour MP Ken Livingstone, who stood as an independent candidate. Two years later, the mayor and his assembly moved into the new City Hall building (below), on the south bank of the Thames near Tower Bridge.

Security

After the terrorist attacks on New York's World Trade Center on September 11, 2001, security (below) was increased throughout London. This is particularly the case at major landmark buildings and airports.

Right: The new footbridge connects Bankside with Upper Thames Street, linking the Tate Modern gallery to St. Paul's.

Left: Ken Livingstone (born 1945) was leader of the former Greater London Council when it was abolished in 1986. Fourteen years later, he was elected mayor.

Millennium Bridge

This pedestrian bridge, situated between Blackfriars and Southwark bridges, is the first new Thames crossing in central London since Tower Bridge opened in 1894. Unfortunately it got off to a poor start: about 80,000 people crossed the 1,082-feet (330 m) bridge on its first day, and the aluminium deck started to wobble. It had to be closed to the public for over a year, while engineers fitted new shock absorbers. These solved the problem and the bridge was finally reopened in 2002.

Millennium Dome

The Dome (below) was intended to be the centerpiece of the UK millennium celebrations, with exhibitions in 15 different zones. It was built on the site of a former gasworks, beside the river in north Greenwich, though many people thought it was too expensive and not viable. The huge Dome, 1,050 feet (320 m) across and 164 feet (50 m) high attracted 6.5 million visitors in 2000, but still closed on the last day of the year. It was thought that it would be turned into a high-tech business park, but in 2003 it was still unclear what the future held for the empty structure.

Right: London's City Hall building.

The Future?

The London cityscape will undoubtedly change, as new buildings alter the skyline. In 2004, the new Swiss Re building is due to open on the site of the old Baltic Exchange, and there are plans to redesign the South Bank. A new National Stadium is being built on the site of the old Wembley Stadium, with a retractable roof supported by a 436-feet (133 m) high arch. London has also decided to put in a bid to host the Olympic Games in 2012.

Index